W9-CCE-543

VERN YIP'S
DESIGN WISE

EUROPE & AFRICA
TASCHEN
ASIA & OCEANIA
TASCHEN

VERN YIP'S DESIGN WISE

YOUR SMART GUIDE TO A BEAUTIFUL HOME

VERN YIP

RUNNING PRESS
PHILADELPHIA • LONDON

To my mom, Vera, for dedicating her life to making me the man that I am.

To my sister, Katherine, for being the best example of a supportive sibling.

To our children, Gavin and Vera, for making me laugh and beam with pride.

And to my husband, Craig, for never failing to lead my cheering section.

Published by Running Press,
An Imprint of Perseus Books, a Division of PBG Publishing, LLC,
A Subsidiary of Hachette Book Group, Inc.

Printed in Canada

ISBN 978-0-7624-5985-8

Library of Congress Control Number: 2016938275

E-book ISBN 978-0-7624-6109-7

9 8 7 6 5 4 3 2
Digit on the right indicates the number of this printing

Designed by Josh McDonnell
Edited by Jennifer Kasius
Typography: Avenir and Brandon

Running Press Book Publishers
2300 Chestnut Street
Philadelphia, PA 19103-4371

Visit us on the web!
www.runningpress.com

CONTENTS

INTRODUCTION:
A WINDING ROAD TO DESIGN

I took a fairly unusual route to become an interior designer. Like many Asian Americans of my generation, my parents made huge sacrifices to come to the United States so that my sister and I could be afforded the best education and the most number of life and career opportunities possible. As immigrants who had to start over in a new and unfamiliar country, my parents saw a great deal of value in a stable profession, and that is what they wanted for me. Specifically, they wanted their only son to be a doctor. The Chinese culture holds medical professionals in very high regard, so they encouraged me in that direction. My mother always said that if she gave me a room full of puppies to choose from, I would pick the sickest one. So perhaps she felt that I had the kind of temperament a doctor needs to be successful. I did my best to honor their wishes and I was, in fact, a pre-med student at the University of Virginia, where I focused on both chemistry and economics. But my heart simply wasn't in it.

When I was at the National Institutes of Health, working in the Transmitted and Transfused Viruses Laboratory, I would find myself looking around the lab thinking, why do the walls have to be this terrible yellow, why is the fluorescent lighting so harsh and unattractive? This made me realize my passion for design was quite strong, and that perhaps I should follow that road.

Two weeks before I was to start medical school, I decided that I had better start listening to what my heart (and my mind) were telling me—which was to pursue what I really felt I was put on earth to do—architecture and design. My mom already knew about my interest, but she hoped that it would become a hobby I'd engage in "on the side." When I told her of my decision to change career paths, she was concerned. However, she quickly came to support my choice. I went on to further my studies and earned an MBA and Master of Architecture from the Georgia Institute of Technology. The MBA was likely a relief to her; it offered a practical alternative to design. She also saw that I applied myself to everything I did. Having such a supportive and encouraging mom has been a big part of my success.

My mom would also have to admit she had a hand in my passion for design. She raised me to have the same deep appreciation for craftsmanship as she did. She understood the difference between something that was well made and a masterpiece, and shared that knowledge with me. Her highly developed aesthetic sense was reflected in how she dressed and presented herself and how she kept the house. All of that had an impact on me and my sister, Katherine. To this day we both still have our hands deep in the world of design. In many ways, my mom was also a rebel—particularly daring for a traditional Chinese woman. She was the first woman to ride a motorcycle through her town, which

was not looked upon kindly. She got in trouble for that. During her time at university, pursuing studies to become a psychiatrist and educator, there were far more men than women, perhaps one woman for every hundred men.

It took particular courage for my parents to leave China and come to America, where my mother and father did not speak the language well or understand the culture. My father, a biochemist, took a job as a busboy at a Marriott in Virginia, and my mother washed floors in a bank. These sacrifices were worth it to them in order to give my sister and me a better life. So perhaps my non-traditional path to design is not so surprising.

Eventually, my parents opened retail stores that sold furniture and home décor items imported from Asia. Like so many kids of immigrants, I worked in the family business. After school, on the weekends, I would pitch in. This is where I really observed and absorbed my mother's artistic bent. She gave me a lot of leeway to explore my own creative interests. I created the jewelry displays for the store starting at a very young age; by the time I was nine, I was creating window displays. Some of them were pretty bad, but she gave me that freedom to learn from my failures—despite the fact that the store was in a very nice part of town, right next to Neiman Marcus. She had faith in me, and that is an amazing feeling.

My unusual educational background (for an interior designer, at least) has given me a great gift in terms of how I work with interior spaces and clients. While I certainly express emotions, whimsy, and creativity in my work, I also bring a deep analytical understanding of structure, scale, and proportion that directs my designs toward being both aesthetically pleasing and practical for the people living in those spaces. I like to explain to a client exactly how I arrive at my decisions, and in the process, teach them information they can use in the future. It's useful to absorb the basic principles of good design that have stood the test of time, regardless of the style you choose. Such knowledge saves money because you know what to ask about and look for when making a major purchase; it saves time because you don't have to agonize about where to put the sofa or place a coffee table. It frees you up to concentrate on developing your eye and your own personal style.

I also have a spouse, two children, and five dogs (make that two very active children and "500 pounds of dogs"). We are on the go all the time, so I understand the parameters of designing and decorating rooms that fit with a busy family life. That's why I purposely chose not to make this a monument to my designs or myself—it's a guide that recognizes life happens, and to that end, shows you how to make your house convey the best version of your personal style and life. Even if you want to put your feet up and eat dinner on your sofa, you will find something relevant in this book. Ditto for people who want to throw elaborate dinner parties, or enjoy sit-down meals around the dining table with their families.

Some decorating books, while very beautiful and inspiring (I have a library of them!), often neglect, talk around, or bury the concrete rules that make spaces work. The book you hold in your hands starts with the hard and fast principles of good design—and makes them completely understandable and accessible. Indeed, this is the overarching philosophy of my design: functional and beautiful. I want to help you figure out how to solve a design dilemma accurately and for good value. You can pick up the book and access what you need to know quickly and easily—nothing crucial is obscured in dense or flowery text. For that reason, some information is repeated when relevant, so you don't have to pause to cross reference important material on another page.

Not only do I offer an in-depth look at the principles of design that make putting a home together less stressful, I give you real examples of how I have applied these tried-and-true principals to create original, beautiful, and very livable rooms in my own homes. My design "calling card," or signature, is attention to detail married with precise, clean-lined interiors, balanced with a sense of warmth. Many elements of my interiors are eclectic and show a love of travel throughout Asia, Latin America, Africa, and Europe.

As each chapter unfolds, you learn not only about the rules of design that actually free you to pursue your aesthetic preferences, but you also learn about how my personal sensibility is brought to life in each of my three homes. Far from being rigid or constraining, the principles of good design—where to place sofas in relation to coffee tables, how high or low to hang artwork, the level at which to install a fixture over a dining table, how large a living room rug should be—are *liberating*. These standards allow you the freedom to focus on developing your personal aesthetic. I hope this approach, combined with design essentials, gives you the confidence to break through "design paralysis" that afflicts too many homeowners.

Ultimately, I believe the client is the most important part of any design project, whether it's someone I've just met for a television show; a private, repeat customer; or you, the reader. I spend as much time as possible getting to know the people I work with, most especially the intricacies and layers of what is important to the homeowner. The goal is to achieve a physical manifestation of the client's point of view, lifestyle, and taste. When a home feels like it has been customized to an owner's functional and aesthetic needs, the people who live there generally find it more appealing than the best five-star resort. Who wouldn't want to come home to something comfortable, delightful, and perfectly tailored to them after a long day?

Since I cannot, unfortunately, get to know all of you, I can only share what I have learned from my own journey developing and honing my style, and from my clients. By delivering a streamlined and, for the most part, clean-lined version of my clients' desires, I have generally protected them from having to live with a space that quickly becomes dated. When rooms are simple and beautiful, and keep the time-tested design principles of balance and scale in mind, it is easy to change one or two elements (color, accessories) to refresh the basic good bones of the room. I believe you can achieve that with this book as your guide.

My goal is to both teach *and* inspire—to balance beauty with wisdom. Like me, the book is equal parts left brain/right brain. In *Part One: The Elements of Smart Design*, the chapters unfold to teach you the rules of design and dimension; what you need to know and consider when making purchasing decisions about fixtures, furnishings, fabrics, and colors; and finally, how to take what you've learned and put it to work as you design and arrange the spaces in your home. Look for sidebar features called "Learn From Vern," which share practical information and tips on achieving personalization. "Cheat Sheets" at the end of the book round up some of the most essential information for easy access. My hope is that you take this book with you when you shop, and use it when working with salespeople, gallery owners, artists and other makers, dealers, designers, craftspeople, and installers. No need to keep all the facts and figures in your head, just look in the book when you're ready to install a towel bar or lay down a rug and create a seating area.

In *Part Two: A Sense of Place*, you'll see—and learn—how I brought design principles together with my own personal style in each of my three homes: an historic Atlanta home; a modern Manhattan apartment; and a casual, laid-back family home on the Gulf Coast of Florida. Each chapter offers expansive images of full rooms and many details—from furnishings to architectural features throughout the homes.

You see, in great detail, how I interpret town, urban, and seaside spaces as I walk you through the rooms in my homes. The images demonstrate how the basic design principles in the first half of the book make the rooms work for an active family with young children and pets—a situation many of you no doubt find yourselves in. The result is what I hope becomes an essential resource for anyone who is decorating, redecorating, renovating, or building his or her dream home.

I think we should learn how to make some design magic, don't you?

PART ONE:

THE ELEMENTS OF SMART DESIGN

The hard and fast principles of good design result in remarkable room transformations—no matter what style you choose or are drawn to. There is no mystery to these rules and principles, nor do they inhibit your creativity. In fact, once you know the right formulas and combinations, or at least have them handy and accessible, you can design any room with great confidence *and* originality. This section takes a scrapbook approach to both visuals and information to give you the design information you need to make whatever style you choose look great—pleasing to the eye and to the body (because you should be comfortable when you sit down with your friends and family); proportional; well-lit; and in color harmony.

As you choose the finishes, furniture, and fixtures, you're also making important style decisions. Design definitely goes through cycles and trends. We have to be careful not to fall into what can be very seductive trend traps. When I was on *Trading Spaces*, Tuscan kitchens and sponge-painted walls were quite popular. I worked with several homeowners on the show who dreamt of installing an "authentic" burnt-orange Tuscan kitchen in their split-level or mid-century ranch. I had to find out what elements of the trend attracted these homeowers to make sure they sincerely loved the look, and weren't just being drawn to it because it was popular. Thankfully, that particular trend isn't as ubiquitous as it once was. The industrial look is another trend, but that too will fade, as people grow weary of its cold, hard surfaces. Some other *design du jour* will take its place.

The best approach in a world filled with the next new thing is to create something timeless and enduring that speaks to your life and personality and tells *your* story. The solution? Surround yourself with quality pieces and personal items that you love and feel passionate about. This path transcends trends, so no matter what the fashion dictates, your home will be a manifestation of you. As long as you follow this approach, your home will never feel dated. Another bonus: When you walk through your front door, you feel *at home*. It becomes your favorite place to be more than any other place on the planet. Everyone deserves to have that feeling.

Achieving that feeling starts with knowing what to buy and where to put it. Once you know how long your sofa needs to be, for instance, you can focus on finding the one that delights your heart, puts a smile on your face, is built to last, *and* feels "right" in the space where you place it. Logistics may not be the most glamorous part of design and decoration, but once you know the facts behind the fancy, selecting pieces that make you happy and that you love becomes fun. No more design paralysis or fear of making the wrong choice.

PORTUGAL

CHAPTER ONE:
DESIGN BY THE NUMBERS

CRITICAL DIMENSIONS FOR TRANSFORMATIVE SPACES

Get past your fear of numbers and get out your calculators and tape measures. What follows are important numbers that make designing and decorating a room much easier and more pleasurable. Knowing the right numbers takes the anxiety out of shopping and pulling a room together. Think of this first chapter as a guide to basic dimensions, which you can build on as you proceed on your design journey. Measurements may not be the most glamorous part of design and decorating, but the application of correct space planning allows your rooms to convey lasting aesthetic integrity and personality. People usually don't get excited about numbers; it's like asking someone to get excited about bookkeeping or taxes. Yet getting the numbers right is so helpful in giving you a roadmap of where to go with furniture and its proper placement.

One of the important lessons I learned from working on television with many different kinds of people with differing budgets and tastes, is that space planning is the great equalizer. It really doesn't matter how much you have to spend—all furniture, no matter its price point, comes in standard dimensions. Your economic situation isn't tied to your personal size requirements for furniture. You can find six- to eight-foot sofas for hundreds of dollars or thousands of dollars. However, the tighter your budget, the more important it is to get measurements right, simply because there is so little room for error. This is another lesson I learned from my years on television, especially on *Trading Spaces*, where we were working with a challenging budget of $1,000 for an entire room. You can create amazing rooms with next to nothing if you understand proportion, dimension, and space.

No matter what design approach you're drawn to—from Colonial to contemporary—or what budget you have, space planning is the first step toward making an empty or awkward space into a smart and beautiful room that reflects you and your family. The basics help your personal style evolve and shine. It's truly remarkable how a carefully placed coffee table can make guests (and you!) feel "right" when sitting on a sofa, and how one that is placed too close or too far away makes socializing awkward and uncomfortable. Likewise, art that is hung incorrectly brings disharmony to a room, when it should be adding aesthetic warmth and character—furthering the "narrative" you are weaving. Good design depends on the quality of the context you create within the spatial parameters that define the room. Our homes provide for our most basic needs: shelter from the elements, a place to prepare and serve food, a place to gather with family and friends, and a place to bathe, dress, and rest in safety and comfort. These are the fundamentals we must honor when we design rooms to serve their intended purposes.

PETER LINDBERGH

SEATING & SEATING AREAS

A seating area that is easy to access and enjoy, and that encourages conversation and comfort, is one of the most important elements in making your home a haven. If you have the right numbers, you can design a space that works, and no one need ever stumble over tables, fall over a couch, trip on electrical cords, or battle other impediments again.

FURNITURE ARRANGEMENTS

Multiple conversation areas can (and should) be established in a single room, especially in large or "great" rooms. Correctly arranging seating and other furniture in living areas is the key to making socializing and relaxing enjoyable and natural, as are the pathways you create within a room to navigate through it.

- **42"** to **120":** The general comfortable distance between seating pieces in a group to establish the most welcoming and functional seating zones. Distances less than 42 inches can feel cramped and invasive of personal space while distances greater than 120 inches make it difficult to hear and converse comfortably without speaking loudly.
- **24"** to **36":** The usual distance needed as passage through a room or between a piece of furniture and an adjacent wall. Although it may be physically possible to pass through a distance less than 24 inches, if you must, your room layout will end up looking crowded and tight.

SOFAS AND SECTIONALS

Americans like a lot of space when they sit down to socialize or relax. Don't fence them in! I really do think it's a cultural thing. Europeans and Asians don't seem to mind as much about converging into one another's personal space, at least in terms of sitting on sofas, as Americans do. That said, personal boundaries with your friends and family are important no matter where you're from, and this should be taken into account when determining the length of a sofa. How many people do you entertain when you host a gathering? Do you plan to use the sofa for stretching out, or lying down and taking a nap? The answers to these questions help determine what you need—along with the amount of space you have in your room to accommodate a sofa or sectional, of course.

THE SEATING NUMBERS YOU NEED TO KNOW

STANDARD SOFA LENGTHS

- **72":** Seats up to 2 people.
- **84":** Seats 2 people comfortably, 3 people who are familiar with each other.
- **96":** Seats 3 people comfortably.
- **108":** Seats 3 comfortably lounging or 4 people sitting upright.
- **120":** Seats 4 people comfortably, although it's rare that 4 people would actually want to sit on the same sofa unless it's a friendly group watching a sporting or entertainment event.

STANDARD SECTIONAL LENGTHS

- **108″** to **168″:** Typical length* of sectional sofas.
- **72″:** Typical length* of the couch component of a small L-shaped sectional. With an attached loveseat depth (or chaise width) at 36 to 42 inches, the overall length measurment results in a small sectional couch ranging from 90 to 114 inches.
- **90″** to **114″:** Typical total length* of a small sectional sofa set. Seats 3 or more.
- **114″** to **138″:** Typical total length* of a mid-size sectional sofa set. Seats 4 or more.
- **138″** to **168″:** Typical total length of a large sectional sofa set. Seats 5 or more.

* Length refers to the longest side of the overall, configured sectional.

STANDARD HEIGHT AND DEPTH CONSIDERATIONS

There is a wide range of seat depths and back heights in the world of sofas, and these measurements do have an impact on how comfortable a sofa will be for an individual. Select the perfect height and depth with your specific needs and room conditions in mind. Here are the numbers you need to know.

- **34″** to **38″:** Typical sofa back height. Lower back heights might not provide enough back support, while taller back heights can look awkward or overwhelming in rooms with ceiling heights lower than 9 feet.
- **34″** to **40″:** Typical overall sofa depth front to back (versus seat depth only). On average, I have found that overall sofa depths in this fairly standard range work well for most people. Deeper sofas (up to 42 inches) are more comfortable for taller individuals and those with long legs. However, those looking for more support might be more comfortable with a depth closer to 36 inches. Those looking for casual lounging and afternoon naps might find a depth closer to 42 inches is just what they need for a truly satisfying snooze.
- **16″** to **20″:** Typical sofa seat height. Sofa seat heights have gotten progressively higher as people have gotten taller and bigger. When purchasing a sofa, make sure that your feet are able to comfortably touch the floor. Remember that sofa seat cushions can compress greatly, depending on cushion composition, so a lower sofa, designed for lounging, won't work well if you will use it in an upright position, or plan to pull it up to a dining room table. You might feel like a kid at the grownup's table.
- **20″** to **24″:** Typical sofa seat depth. Seat depth can range widely, since new sofa designs seemingly continue to get deeper each year. Shorter individuals or people who have shorter legs will generally be more comfortable with a seat depth between 19 to 21 inches, whereas taller or long-legged individuals will be more comfortable with deeper seats closer to 22 to 24 inches. As with most upholstered seating it's best to try it out before purchasing.
- **23″** to **26″:** Typical sofa arm height. As with other elements of a sofa, there are a variety of arm heights and styles, but most that are meant to support your arm will fall within this range. Some sofa styles have arms at the same height as the back. In these instances, you obviously won't be able to rest your arm comfortably on it, so keep this in mind. This style of arm might also not be ideal for those who use the arm to support their head during sofa naps or while reading in a reclining position.

ARMCHAIRS & OTTOMANS

Comfortable, upholstered chairs are a real asset in a living space—they break up the monolithic look of a large sofa or sectional, and many people prefer sitting in a cozy armchair for conversing, reading, or engaging in other hobbies, from reading the *Washington Post* to knitting or mending tasks.

- **36″** x **36″:** Typical armchair width and depth dimensions. What's most comfortable will depend on the user. For the average person, dimensions smaller than this might feel more like an occasional chair; much deeper dimensions might lack sufficient support while much wider dimensions (the ubiquitous "chair and a half") might threaten to overtake many spaces.
- **16″** to **20″:** Typical seat height of an upholstered easy or club chair.
- **12″:** The minimum distance a pair of armchairs can comfortably sit apart in a seating arrangement.
- **12″:** The ideal distance between a lounge chair and an ottoman paired with it. This distance allows you to easily slip into a chair while being close enough to prop your feet up on an ottoman.
- **24″:** The space needed between two armchairs to fit a small cocktail or "drinks" table between them.
- **42″** to **120″:** The space between seating options (couch, arm chairs) to help conversation flow without making people and furniture feel either too crowded or too far apart.
- **16″** to **18″:** Typical height of an ottoman, which means they can be paired well with most armchairs. However, because ottomans are so versatile, manufacturers have started to make them in a wide range of heights, widths, and depths to make them more functional for use as stand-ins for coffee tables and extra seating. So just make sure your ottoman hits the right height for your chair so you can put your feet up, kick back, and relax in comfort. In general, your ottoman should never be higher than the height of the seat you're pairing it with.

LEARN FROM VERN

SOFA SEAT CUSHIONS

Sofa cushions generally come in three styles: bench (single), two-cushion, or three-cushion. In general, I'm not a big fan of the two-cushion style since three people will rarely sit on a sofa that visually looks like it's for two people. Moreover, the two-cushion sofa creates an undesirable "gap" between the two cushions, an uncomfortable area generally avoided by everyone. Sofas that are 84 inches or less benefit from a single cushion; it's an elegant, clean solution. For sofas longer than 84 inches, three cushions are more inviting for three people, and certainly quite comfortable for two people. It's also easier to flip and maintain three cushions than one cushion, which can become unwieldy at longer sofa lengths.

Hotel Book

COFFEE & ACCESSORY TABLES

COFFEE TABLE MEASUREMENTS

Size matters: A coffee table can become a major focal point in a space due to its fairly central location in a room, and because it's highly functional. It can be a place to put your feet up in lieu of an ottoman, or it can become an impromptu dining surface, not to mention a place to hold books and objects.

- **15″** to **18″:** Height of typical coffee tables.
- **0″** to **2″:** The ideal height above or below the sofa or chair seat when placing a coffee table in a seating area. A coffee table should generally be the same as, or within two inches of, the seat height of adjacent chairs and sofas. This helps ensure that the table is convenient for reaching items or for propping your feet on it.
- **20″** to **24″:** Ideal height for a coffee table convenient for serving food and beverages.
- **3″** to **6″:** The ideal height above the sofa when pairing a coffee table with sofa seat when the coffee table will be used frequently for serving coffee and tea. A higher table makes the rituals of pouring and serving much more comfortable.

COFFEE TABLE LENGTHS AND DIAMETERS

Coffee table lengths should never exceed sofa lengths. When this happens, not only are sofas more difficult to access, but you run the risk of banging into coffee table corners more often. Ideally, your coffee table length should be about two-thirds the length of your sofa, except for round tables, which can be more challenging to pair with sofas. Coffee tables can be as small as one-half the overall sofa length but I find that coffee tables this proportionally small are not nearly as functional or visually balanced. You certainly do not want your coffee table to be longer than your sofa, and you do not want it to be too diminutive compared to the sofa's overall dimensions. For ease, here are ideal coffee table lengths for most standard length sofas. Note that once you go beyond a 72-inch sofa, a round table will be difficult to accommodate seamlessly into your seating arrangement:

- **72″ sofa:** 48″ coffee table length, or 36″ to 48″ diameter for a round table
- **84″ sofa:** 56″ coffee table length
- **96″ sofa:** 64″ coffee table length
- **108″ sofa:** 72″ coffee table length
- **120″ sofa:** 80″ coffee table length

COFFEE TABLE DEPTHS

You're often better off using rectangular or oval coffee tables in narrow rooms simply because they fit and function better in these kinds of spaces. Coffee tables shallower than 18 inches aren't always optimally functional or accommodating.

- **18″** to **28″:** Depth of most rectangular or oval coffee tables.
- **36″** to **42″:** Diameter of most round coffee tables, although larger coffee tables with a diameter of 48 inches or more can also be found.

COFFEE TABLE CRITICAL DISTANCES

- **18″:** The ideal distance between the edge of seating and your coffee table, allowing comfortable access to books, remotes, food, and drinks. Distances smaller than this make it hard to get in and out of your seating, while larger distances make it inconvenient to reach the coffee table surface.
- **24″** to **36″:** The minimum comfortable clear distance that you will need to circulate around your coffee table when there's not adjacent seating. 36 inches is a good standard distance for most people and most situations. If you have tighter circumstances, 24 inches is acceptable—but not necessarily comfortable—for a lot of people. Anything fewer than 24 inches is difficult for easy and comfortable passage.

ACCESSORY TABLE MEASUREMENTS

The ideal accessory table, which can include both end tables and side tables, is a convenient surface for putting down items such as a drink or a book. This makes them literally at hand.

- **0″** to **4″:** Typical height above the arm of the chair or sofa beside it. An accessory table can be up to 2 inches below the adjacent sofa or chair, but it can be more awkward to use.
- **2″:** Distance between the outside edge of the sofa or chair that is beside it. This gives it a bit of breathing room so that your furniture doesn't feel slammed together.
- **8″** to **10″:** Typical height above the seat of the armless sofa or chair beside it. This ensures that the table top is still comfortably accessible.

TELEVISIONS

The ideal distance between your media or television screen and the primary seating area from which you watch it is at least partially dependent on the technology of your screen and how big it is. Today's television screens are largely HDTVs with 1080p resolution (also known as Full HD—these TVs have 1080 horizontal lines of vertical resolution). A good rule of thumb for viewing distances is roughly 1.5 to 2.5 times the diagonal measurement of your screen. Seating areas closer than a 1.5 multiplier to your screen size may cause you to notice a breakdown in your picture quality. Seating areas farther than 2.5 times the screen size may be too far for you to be fully engaged with the picture. Some sample viewing distance ranges are shown below for typical television screen sizes:

- **25″ screen:** 38″ to 62″
- **30″ screen:** 45″ to 75″
- **32″ screen:** 48″ to 80″
- **37″ screen:** 56″ to 92″
- **40″ screen:** 60″ to 100″
- **46″ screen:** 69″ to 115″
- **50″ screen:** 75″ to 125″
- **55″ screen:** 83″ to 137″
- **60″ screen:** 90″ to 150″
- **65″ screen:** 98″ to 162″
- **70″ screen:** 105″ to 175″
- **75″ screen:** 74″ to 187″
- **80″ screen:** 120″ to 200″
- **84″ screen:** 126″ to 210″

LEARN FROM VERN

TECH STYLE

A television is what it is, and these days it does not have to be excused or disguised. The newest flat screen televisions are actually quite beautiful: sleek, clean, and simple. They often have invisible frames, or they are frameless. Some even have an elegant curve that supposedly enhances viewing. This is one reason why designers no longer hide televisions behind bulky cabinets—so no need to measure for one! If you prefer to hide your screen, understand all its measurements before searching for the right piece of furniture to accommodate it. You can also hide televisions behind shallow folding doors or a built in.

BATHROOMS

Bathrooms are one of the most used and abused rooms in your home, yet they can, or should be, a serene and relaxing retreat to escape to for a few moments each day. With that in mind, it is crucial for your bathroom to be functional, beautiful, and enjoyable. Here are the numbers you need to know to make your bathroom work:

- **29″** to **32″:** Standard height for conventional bathroom vanities. This always increases by about an inch once the countertop is installed, since most standard countertops are about one-inch thick.
- **33″** to **36″:** Standard height for "back saver" bathroom vanities, plus an inch for the countertop. In recent years, many people have started to prefer these higher bathroom counters and pedestal sinks for their ease of use. Keep in mind small children may find it difficult to reach the sink in taller vanities without the help of a stepstool.
- **75″** to **80″:** Standard height of sconces above bathroom mirrors, measured above the finished floor to the center of the fixture.
- **60″** to **65″:** Standard height of sconces installed on either side of the mirror or medicine cabinet, measured above the finished floor to the center of the fixture. The idea is to install side sconces at eye level, so depending on the heights of the people using the bathroom, some slight adjustments to this rule may be necessary.
- **26″** to **28″:** Standard height of a toilet paper holder, to prevent awkward stretching and reaching.
- **48″:** Standard height of towel bars. This makes towels easy to grab as you step out of the shower—and prevents extra-long towels, like bath sheets, from hitting the floor.
- **29″** to **30″:** Standard height of a bathroom counter when paired with a vessel sink. When using a bowl-style vessel sink, which sits on top of the bathroom counter, bathroom counter height can vary depending on the height of the vessel you choose. If the vessel sink is tall, the 29- or 30-inch cabinet height balances the taller sink. If the vessel sink is low and wide, it is better to choose a back-saver vanity.
- **75″** to **76″:** Typical rod hanging height for a standard shower curtain from finished floor to the center of the rod. Standard shower curtains are typically 72 inches in length, but you should always double check the measurements before you buy. A shower curtain should hang at least 3 to 4 inches above the floor to allow for drainage and cleaning.
- **6″** to **12″:** Ideal distance from the ceiling line to the top of a custom shower curtain. A custom shower curtain can provide a more dramatic statement in a shower or shower-tub combo by hanging closer to the ceiling line, creating a greater sense of height in your bathroom. Like an off-the-shelf shower curtain, the bottom should end 3-4″ above the floor to allow for drainage and cleaning. The inner vinyl liner would hang at the standard height on a separate rod and would be hidden by the rod holding the outer fabric shower curtain.

EAT BY THE NUMBERS

KITCHENS

In a well-designed kitchen and bath, function trumps all. These are spaces where, for safety and efficiency, everything must be of the size and scale that is most practical and user-friendly.

- **36″:** The most comfortable kitchen counter height for most people to stand and work. Under-the-counter appliances, such as a standard dishwasher, fit neatly under this height.
- **24″ x 34.5″:** Standard base cabinet depth and height.
- **12″:** Standard wall cabinet depth. Heights will vary.
- **16″** to **18″:** The ideal clearance distance between the countertop and the wall cabinets. Be aware that some wall cabinets have recessed bottoms to accommodate puck lighting, so make sure you are measuring the clear, usable distance to get placement right. Anything less than 16 inches looks insignificant in relation to cabinets. It's also impractical—you are unable to fit many counter top appliances (coffee maker, blender) within that space. These measurements also give you enough space to conveniently wipe up kitchen splashes.
- **42″:** Minimum kitchen clearance distance between range and opposite base cabinets.
- **36″:** Minimum kitchen clearance distance between dishwasher and opposite base cabinets.
- **42″:** Minimum kitchen clearance distance between a dishwasher and a range on opposing sides. This gives you ample space to open both doors of these appliances at the same time.
- **4″:** The minimum height of a kitchen backsplash. Anything lower than 4 inches would not be ample enough to protect your wall from splashes. Personally I'm not a fan of 4-inch backsplashes because I don't like the way they visually break up the area created by the counter and upper cabinets. For me, backsplash height is best dictated by the space between the counter and the bottom of the wall cabinets. I like to aesthetically address the entire space with one stone or tile material or other washable material. While I don't particularly like wall cabinets, I understand that they are sometimes necessary for storage and function. A visually unified surface between those cabinets and the countertop helps create an unbroken line. However, near wet areas and range tops, I advise installing the backsplash material as far up as possible to protect the wall and for ease of cleaning. A full-width backsplash also allows the eye to flow from one space to the next.
- **0″:** Distance from the top of your cabinet to the ceiling or bottom of a wall soffit. I understand some people may have very high ceilings in their kitchens, making ceiling height cabinets impractical. However, if you have 12-foot ceilings or lower, the cabinets should come as close to the ceiling as possible not only for valuable extra storage, but also to keep the top of the cabinets from becoming cluttered dust catchers.

Counter Intelligence

The material you choose for your countertops is important not only in terms of style, but practicality as well. Here's a quick guide to the strength and stain and scratch resistance of the most popular countertop materials. Use this information when choosing surfaces for the kitchen, bath, laundry room, or any other space where a sturdy counter is required, including all sorts of tables. The first chart is organized from what I think is the least durable to the most durable material. The second chart is based on actual relative density of the material, from softest to hardest.

1. Non-Stone Surfaces

Type	Stain Resistant	Scratch Resistant	Heat Resistant	Basic Care
Sealed* Butcher Block	Yes	No	No	Can be sanded and resealed as necessary. Scratches must be oiled or sealed. Harder than stainless.
Laminate**	Yes	No	No	Use non abrasive cleansers and with a soft cloth.
Stainless Steel	Yes	No	Yes	Wipe with a soft, damp cloth and mild cleanser.
Solid Surface (i.e., Corian)	Yes	No	No	Can be sanded to remove scratches. Clean with a soft, damp cloth and mild cleanser.
Sealed* Concrete	Yes	Yes	Yes	To avoid stains, proper sealing and waxing is required. Potentially harder than stainless but more brittle.

2. Sealed* natural stone surfaces

Type	Stain Resistant	Scratch Resistant	Heat Resistant	Basic Care
Sealed* Soapstone	Yes	No	Yes	Must be oiled with mineral oil on a regular basis to maintain shine. Maintenance of edges to eliminate any scratches or chips may be required.
Sealed* Limestone	Yes	No	Yes	Must be sealed regularly to prevent staining and pitting.
Sealed* Marble	Yes	No	Yes	Must be sealed to prevent staining.
Granite	Yes	Yes	Yes	Must be sealed regularly to avoid surface damage.
Quartz (Cambria)***	Yes	Yes	Yes	Regular cleaning with a soft cloth and mild cleanser.

* Unsealed natural materials are less stain resistant. Be sure to reseal as needed.

** High-end laminates are potentially more scratch resistant. Quality counts.

** 93% Quartz

The Garden Book
Remodelista
WINDOWS

DINING ROOMS

DINING TABLES

- **28″** to **31″:** The standard height of a dining table, but 30 inches is the most common height. This is also the standard height of most desks, so in small spaces, a desk can do double-duty as a dining table, likewise a dining room can function as a home office when not in use. Desks are not as deep as dining tables, so dinner with friends may feel even more intimate.

TABLE LENGTH OR DIAMETER FOR COMFORTABLE SEATING

Use the chart to determine the length in inches (for rectangular and oval) or diameter in inches (for round) of the table you need for seating your maximum number of guests. These dimensions provide comfortable seating in chairs 20 inches wide for the number of guests indicated. For rectangular tables only, the capacity for each size includes figures for arrangements that include guests at each end of the table.

Shape	36″	48″	54″	60″	72″	84″	96″	108″	120″
Rectangular**	1 to 2	4	4 to 6	4 to 6	6 to 8	6 to 8	8 to 10	10	10 to 12
Round/Square	2	4	6	6 to 8	8 to 10	10 to 12	n/a*	n/a*	n/a*
Oval**	n/a*	n/a*	n/a*	6	6 to 8	8	n/a*	n/a*	n/a*

* Not applicable, as these are non-standard measurements for these shapes of tables.

** Assuming standard depth is 36″ to 42″.

IDEAL DINING SEATING SPACING

Once you have determined the shape and size of your table, use the following measurements to ensure the comfort of your guests when they are seated.

Clearance and Distance in Inches for Maximum Comfort at Table

- **24":** The centerline-to-centerline space between dining chairs at a rectangular table.
- **7":** Between the chair arm and the lowest point on the table top including the apron* of the table.
- **12":** Minimum place setting space in front of each diner at a rectangular table.
- **15":** Maximum centerpiece height to allow diners at the table to see each other.
- **26":** The centerline-to-centerline space between dining chairs at a round table.
- **29" to 31":** Standard height for a dining room table.
- **36":** Minimum distance from the outer edge or width of a dining table to the edge of the rug underneath.
- **48":** Minimum distance between dining table and an exit.
- **54":** Minimum distance from the table's edge to the nearest wall or piece of furniture, when a chair sits in between; otherwise maintain a minimum distance of 24 to 36 inches.
- **36":** Height of a hanging fixture's underside to the top of a table surface.

* An upper rail or carved panel that extends directly below the main table top and that sits above the diners' legs. On tables with corner legs, the apron extends between the legs of the table.

DINING ROOM CHAIRS

- **19":** The standard seat height for a dining room chair. However, there are variations in this, as you can find dining chairs with seat heights ranging from 18 to 20 inches. The height of your chairs relates to the height of your dining table, and even one inch can make a difference in how you feel at the table. Take this into consideration when pairing a dining table with chairs. For example, if you have a taller seat, say 20 inches, and your table is on the low side, say 29 inches, diners may feel awkward.
- **11"** to **13":** The space between a dining seat and the table top, depending on the height and what makes most people sitting at the table comfortable.
- **18"** to **20":** The height of extra chairs and pull up seating for dining. When pulling up extra seating to a dining table, keep these measurements in mind. Garden stools, benches, side chairs not meant for dining, settees, and even sofas may be too low for practical use at a dining table.

STOOLS

Today's casual lifestyle has created demand for alternatives to the traditional dining room and the traditional dining table. The kitchen counter has become a gathering place, homework space, and of course, a spot to grab a quick bite, or even to serve a three-course meal to guests. However you use the counter, maximize the comfort and utility of its seating with these dimensions.

- **10"** to **12":** The typical distance from the seat to the top of the counter or table. This allows most people enough room to get in and out of the seat comfortably.
- **18"** to **20":** Typical table stool seat height to work with a typical 30-inch dining table.
- **24"** to **26":** Typical counter stool seat height to work with typical 36-inch counter height.
- **30"** to **32":** Typical bar stool seat height to work with the typical bar height of 42 inches.
- **34"** to **36":** Typical spectator stool seat height to fit an extra tall bar height of 46 inches.

LEARN FROM VERN

CUSTOM LOOK CABINETS AT AN OFF-THE-RACK PRICE

If you want a more modern and comfortable 36″ height for a bathroom counter, there may not be a need to special order a custom bathroom cabinet. A base kitchen cabinet, which has a standard height of 35 inches, will be 36 inches high once you add a countertop. It's a smart and affordable solution. Kitchen cabinets come in a wide variety of styles and finishes, so your bathroom will have a custom look without the custom price. If you do use a base kitchen cabinet in the bathroom, keep in mind that the standard depth is 24 inches instead of the standard 18 inches for a bathroom counter, so you *will* need to make sure your bathroom can accommodate the extra inches. You can also use kitchen countertops to top it off, whether they are made to order or off the rack.

COMFORTABLE COUNTER SEATING

Counter-height and bar-height stools can benefit from a little more horizontal spacing than is usually allotted for table-height stools and dining chairs because they can be more difficult to scoot in and out of. Allow 28 inches per counter- or bar-height stool for an adequate amount of space for someone to slide in and out of without necessarily having to fully pull the stool out. To determine the proper number of stools, measure the amount of space you're working with in inches and divide by 28. For example, if your counter is 9½ feet long or about 112 inches, you could fit up to four barstools comfortably at that counter. Supporting brackets under a table or countertop may prevent you from having as many stools as this formula dictates, since they often take up leg space.

SLEEP BY THE NUMBERS

BEDS

Of course, the most important part of your bed is your mattress. It's not possible to select a bed frame without first deciding what size mattress you're going to use. Selecting the right mattress size typically depends on two things: comfort and space. It will be important to space plan your bedroom to ensure that you can fit the bed size you think the sleeper or sleepers will get the best night's rest in.

STANDARD U.S. MATTRESS SIZES

- **39″ W x 75″ L:** Twin/single, designed for one person.
- **39″ W x 80″ L:** Twin extra-long, designed for one person. Popularly found in college dormitories and good for taller single sleepers.
- **54″ W x 75″ L:** Full/double/standard. Originally designed to accommodate two people many decades ago. This size is now more commonly used for a single sleeper or for couples with very tight bedrooms.
- **60″ W x 80″ L:** Queen, the most popular size in the U.S., accommodating two average-size people comfortably or a single person very generously.
- **76″ W x 80″ L:** King/eastern king. Many couples prefer the extra width of this bed so that each person can have his/her own space.
- **72″ W x 84″ L:** California king. This bed is 4 inches narrower than a standard king, so even if you aren't looking for the extra length, saving 4 inches of width is helpful if your bed wall is narrow. This is also the longest of the standard bed sizes, so make sure you have the right depth in your room so there's room to walk around the end of the bed. California kings are good options for tall individuals who need the extra length, or for couples where one or more of the individuals need or want the extra length.

BEDS BY THE NUMBERS

- **24″** to **36″:** Passage space around your bed is important to keep in mind when determining the size of your bed. You will need a minimum of 24 inches of passage space around the sides and foot of your bed frame, unless you are pressing your bed up against a wall, which is not recommended unless you have no other options. Typically, you will want a minimum closer to 30 to 36 inches of passage space around the sides and foot of the bed for comfort. Larger individuals will likely prefer even more.
- **17″** to **18″:** Platform beds and their mattresses generally end up with a combined height (platform + mattress) of 17 to 18 inches above the finished floor. This is close to the height of most sofa seats so if your bedroom doesn't have room to accommodate extra seating, a platform bed is a good option because it offers a comfortable sitting height, so handy for putting on or taking off shoes.
- **2″:** The amount of space I recommend between the headboard and the wall. This will extend the life of both your wall and headboard while providing plug heads with necessary room for outlets behind the bed.
- **24″** to **26″:** For most typical mattresses, the average measurement from the finished floor to the height of the combined bed frame and mattress. Because of innovations in sleep technology, there are a wide variety of mattress heights available today, from standard mattresses to fluffy pillow tops, and from extra deep to high-density foam mattresses. How high would you be comfortable with for both sleeping and sitting on the edge of the bed? Understanding how the general type of mattress you're buying will affect that height is important.
- **36″ or higher:** Many traditional and antique beds have a combined frame and mattress height that puts the top of mattress at this higher level. You might need help in the form of a step stool to climb into bed!

MUSEUM
ANIMAL STORIES
FAIRY TALES
FAIRY STORIES

HEADBOARDS

- **48":** The average height of a headboard from the floor to the top edge. This leaves about 24 inches from the top of the average mattress to the top of the headboard—enough room to lean back comfortably and read this book. If you're often in a seated position in bed, make sure you have at least 4 to 5 inches from the top of your head to the top of the headboard. This will ensure that you're comfortable in this position. Measure the height of your mattress from the finished floor and add this to the measurement of your waist to your head. Add 4 to 5 inches to this measurement for your ideal headboard height. As long as you stick to the minimum measurement of 24 inches, you can go higher. Some headboards go right up to the ceiling to create what can be a very dramatic effect. In this situation, the headboard becomes the centerpiece of the room. For safety, securely fasten very tall headboards to the wall, *not* the bed frame.

DRESSERS

A dresser or two are obvious choices for bedrooms, as they are a convenient and accessible way to store clothing. Properly folded or rolled clothing actually do better at staying in shape and wrinkle free than clothes on hangers jammed into a full closet. However, a dresser's usefulness extends beyond the bedroom. They are great in entryways, living areas, and even dining rooms, especially those that may be too small to hold a conventional sideboard or buffet. Whatever space you plan to place a dresser, measurements are important to maintain balance and scale in a room. To help you understand the often-confusing terminology about dressers, the following guidelines should make it easier to determine which style suits your space.

- **Dresser, Bureau, Waist High or Lowboy:**
  - 36" to 48" wide
  - 18" to 24" deep
  - 29" to 37" high
- **Chest of Drawers, Gentleman's Chest or Highboy:**
  - 30" to 40" wide
  - 18" to 24" deep
  - 42" to 56" high
- **Double Dresser:**
  - 60" to 72" wide
  - 18" to 24" deep
  - 26" to 34" high
- **Lingerie Chest:**
  - 22" to 24" wide
  - 16" to 18" deep
  - 50" to 54" high
- **Armoire or Wardrobe:**
  - 32" to 68" wide
  - 17" to 24" deep
  - 60" to 76" high

LEARN FROM VERN

STAY SLIM IN TIGHT SPACES

For super tight bedrooms, keep your bed on a simple wood or metal frame that does not exceed the width of your mattress and select a thinner headboard, whether it is upholstered or hard, and that can be easily mounted onto the wall. Standard headboards that attach to a bed frame usually take up anywhere from 6 to 12 inches, so you can save yourself up to 10 inches by using this trick.

DON'T GET STUCK

The king-size headboard is among the most difficult pieces of furniture to move into a bedroom, particularly if it is tall. If you are planning on a king bed frame, measure your hallways, stairs, door openings, turning radiuses, and elevators (where applicable) to ensure that your king headboard can make it into the intended bedroom. Unlike king mattresses (which bend) and king box springs (which can be purchased as two twins), king headboards are unforgiving, so take your measurements before purchasing your bed frame.

MIX IT OR MATCH IT

Don't feel you must match your nightstands. In fact, it's a nice textural element, and a personalized one, to choose two different styles with similar dimensions with one unifying factor, like color or material. For instance, if you are super tidy, you might place a simple walnut table on your side of the bed and your (messier) spouse might find a small or low-slung walnut dresser with multiple drawers more practical. Keep table heights similar, especially if you plan to use them with a pair of matching lamps. No matter what kinds of lamps you use, the tops of the lampshades should be at about the same height when placed on either side of the bed.

NIGHTSTANDS

- **0″** to **2″:** The space between your nightstand and your bed—easy enough to reach for a glass of water or the alarm clock. A surface that sits below your mattress height can be more difficult to access.
- **25″ or less:** The ideal nightstand depth—any deeper and you might have trouble getting in and out of bed without bumping into the table! Ouch.
- **0″** to **2″:** The height above the top of a mattress a table surface should sit if you choose to use a shelf, drop leaf table, or an accessory table as a bedside surface.

  The bigger the bed, the bigger the nightstand. For a king-size bed, consider a two-door cabinet or even a three-drawer chest (as long as it's the right depth). For a twin or double bed, look for a "leggy" table or a properly scaled storage piece that won't overwhelm smaller bed sizes.

LIGHTING BY THE NUMBERS

Four walls do not a room make. A room's purpose determines the measurements and dimensions for its ceilings fixtures and other forms of lighting, from task-related to purely aesthetic. Here are my guidelines for the kind of illumination I use most frequently in my homes and in my designs.

RECESSED LIGHTING

Down light, pot light, can light—call them whatever you want, but by any name, recessed lighting in my opinion is essential both for overall ambiance and for specific tasks that vary from room to room. A popular rule of thumb is to divide your ceiling height in half and use that distance to determine centerline-to-centerline spacing for recessed fixtures. Rooms with taller ceilings can tolerate spacing that is farther apart; when in doubt, though, err on the side of installing too many lights rather than too few.

- **18″:** The distance that recessed lights should be from the walls to the light's centerline.
- **6″:** The diameter of the most common standard can light fixture; the size used most frequently by builders because it's economical, i.e., less expensive than smaller alternatives. In my opinion, 6 inches is too big and too visually distracting.
- **4″:** The diameter of a can lighting fixture that I believe is less distracting among affordable can lighting options. I prefer 4-inch can fixtures for this reason. They are usually slightly more expensive than 6-inch cans, however, as lighting technology advances, 4-inch cans are becoming much more popular and accessible. Three-inch can fixtures are also gaining in popularity among designers and others.

DISTANCE BETWEEN EACH RECESSED LIGHT

- **36″:** In kitchens, recessed lights above workspaces should be placed about 36 inches apart for maximum task illumination.
- **Distance formula:** $\frac{\text{ceiling height}}{2} = \text{Centerline to Centerline Distance}$
- **48″:** In living areas with 8-foot ceilings, install recessed lights about every 48 inches around the perimeter of the ceiling for optimal illumination.
- **60″:** In living areas with 10-foot ceilings, install recessed lights about every 60 inches around the perimeter of the ceiling.

SCONCES

Sconces provide elegant lighting for all manner of decor. I don't think sconces are essential or necessary lighting, but they are effective in certain situations. For example, in bathrooms at a vanity, or flanking a mirror, they are quite useful. Use scones for general or accent lighting, or purely for decoration. Unless the bulb is a design feature, place the sconce so that its bulb is not visible. The distance between sconces varies depending on their intended purpose.

- **60″** to **72″:** The general placement height for a wall sconce from the floor to the center of sconce. A sconce should not be placed below eye level or so high that it competes with recessed lighting or pendants unless they are being used as nightstand lighting.
- **24″** to **36″:** The minimum suggested clear distance between sconces. For example, a 12-foot wall could have at least two sconces occupying the center of the wall but no closer than 36 inches from each other.
- **48″:** The distance sconces used as general light sources should be from one another for optimum illumination.
- **60″** to **65″:** The general height of a bathroom sconce adjacent to a mirror measured from finished floor to its center.
- **75″** to **80″:** The general height of a bathroom sconce above a mirror measured from finished floor to its center.

PENDANTS & HANGING FIXTURES

No other form of lighting combines the utility and design possibilities of the pendant, or hanging, fixture. From glittering chandeliers to dramatic spotlights, pendant lighting enhances both a room's purpose and its aesthetic appeal.

CRITICAL DISTANCES FOR PENDANT AND HANGING FIXTURES

Always measure from the pendant's lowest point.

- **66":** Measurement when placing a pendant above the dining room table, desk, library table, game table, or any other 29 to 30 inch high table you will be seated at, from the finished floor to the lowest point of the fixture. This allows for proper illumination of the table surface while still allowing people to see each other across the table. Also note that, for tables up to 6 feet in length, one fixture is sufficient. Tables that exceed 72 inches may need multiple fixtures with separate junction boxes or a single fixture that spans the correct length of the table to adequately illuminate the surface of the table.

  The size and shape of your table determines the lighting fixture or fixtures. Fixtures above a round table should never exceed the diameter of the table itself. For rectangular or ovals tables, single or multiple fixtures should not exceed three-quarters of the overall length of the table, including chairs, nor the overall width of the table. Alternatively, if the table does not have chairs at its head and foot, the fixtures may run its entire length.

- **36"** to **40":** Measurement when placing pendants over a kitchen island, from top of island countertop to underside of fixture, to allow for illumination and unobstructed visibility.

- **6":** Measurement when placing a hanging fixture over a bed, the fixture should be 6 inches above head level when seated in your bed. Because bed frame and mattress heights vary significantly, there is no exact measurement that can be given without these components in place. Hanging fixtures with a minimum of 6 inch of head clearance, when you are in a seated position in your bed, keeps you from bumping it accidentally.

- **76"** to **78":** The minimum measurement in a hallway or other open space, from finished floor to the lowest point of the fixture, to allow for comfortable passage for most homes with ceilings that are 114 inches (9 feet, 6 inches) or lower.

- **84":** For ceiling heights at or greater than 114 inches (or 9 feet, 6 inches), hang fixtures at 84 inches from finished floor to the lowest point to ensure complete ease for all but a few people. It's not so high that the light is not functional, and the light stays in proportion to the height of the room. Hanging fixtures higher than this height do not allow the fixture to be appreciated and keeps the light too high. Of course, there are always exceptions, i.e., when you have a double story entryway or room, or ceilings that are higher than 14 feet. You may have to adjust accordingly.

LAMPS AND SHADES

- **58″** to **66″:** The total combined height of the table and the table lamp or a floor lamp measured from the bottom of the table (or floor lamp) to the top of the lampshade, not including the finial. This measurement usually allows proper illumination when seated on a sofa or chair adjacent to the lamp, and prevents having to look into the bulb from either a seated or standing position in most situations.

- **Chin Level:** For a bedside lamp to illuminate reading properly, the bottom of the lampshade should generally be at your chin level when you are sitting up in bed. Because mattress, bed frame, and nightstand heights very greatly, the easiest way to get a bedside lamp at the right height is to have those other components in place first. In instances where the lamp is too low, a stack of books wider than the base of the lamp creates a plinth for the lamp to sit on, elevating it to the desired height and saving you from having to go get another lamp.

SELECTING THE PERFECT LAMP SHADE

Make sure you choose a shade designed to fit the base of your lamp base. The bottom of the lampshade should land about midway on the neck of the lamp base. The switch should never be visible on a lamp, unless you are dealing with a pull chain. If it falls into the socket area, it should be fully hidden by the lampshade.

THE PROPER HEIGHT:

- **Table or Bedside Lamp:** In general, a lampshade should never be taller than the lamp base measured from the bottom of the base to the middle of the neck, unless the lampshade and base have been intentionally designed to emphasize the shade height. A shade should measure about ⅓ of the overall lamp height, and the base should be about ⅔ of the overall lamp height.

- **Floor Lamp:** The shade should be about ⅓ of the overall lamp height, and the lamp base will be about ⅔. At a minimum, the shade should reach halfway down the neck (if there is one) and fully cover the socket and harp.

THE PROPER WIDTH:

- **Table and Bedside Lamp Shade:** In general, the diameter should be within 2 inches (greater or smaller) of the overall lamp base height, measured from the bottom of the lamp base to the underside of the socket, including the lamp base neck.

- **Floor Lamp Shade:** In general, the diameter should not exceed twice the width of the widest part of the floor lamp base.

ART & MIRRORS BY THE NUMBERS

No discussion of space is complete without considering the objects we affix to them. Whether you are a fan of 19th century American prints or African tribal art, the design principles do not vary:

- **60″:** The optimal height for hanging pictures and mirrors on walls without other architectural features. Measure from the floor to the center of the piece for a pleasing eye-level view. When hanging groups of images and/or mirrors, think of the height and width of all pictures, and use the center point of the group to calculate your 60-inch measurement. Lay the composition on the floor first, taking into consideration your wall measurements, to find the center point. Then transfer that calculation and layout to the wall.
- **2″:** The minimum distance between the bottom of the frame to the top of a chair rail, mantel, or headboard.
- **2″:** The minimum space you should leave between artwork and/or mirrors hung in groupings.

LEARN FROM VERN

ADDING A WINDOW

For rooms that don't benefit from a lot of natural light or that just need brightening, hang a large mirror on the wall opposite a window. The natural light entering your room through that window hits the mirrored surface, and bounces it back into the space. Without the mirror, the light would just be absorbed into the wall. This is the quickest and least expensive way of adding another "window" to a room. Aside from elevating the light level, it has the added benefit of doubling the view out of your window.

AREA RUGS BY THE NUMBERS

Area rugs are a decorator's dream: they define spaces within a larger space; they anchor furniture so that a room "reads" correctly to the eye; and they can make a room appear larger when properly sized. To keep your dream from becoming a nightmare, you also need a tape measure to make sure the size of the rug is such that it fits the room in which you placed it, and can do the job you have assigned it, i.e., defining a conversation space, filling an entire room, or accenting a small area. Here are the general rules:

- **12"** to **18":** The best distance between an area rug and at least one wall is between 12 inches and 18 inches so that a foot to a foot and a half of flooring is visible—otherwise it might look like wall-to-wall carpeting that did not quite make it. In very large rooms, you can go up to 24 inches between wall and rug.
- **36":** A dining area rug should span about 36 inches wider on all sides of a dining table to allow chairs to pull out easily without catching on the edge. If this isn't possible, it might be better to forgo an area rug here altogether.
- **1":** Alternatively, if you do want to "carpet" a room with an area rug instead of installing wall-to-wall carpeting, ensure your bound rug comes within an inch of the baseboard all around the room.
- At a minimum, the front legs of your sofa and chairs should sit on an area rug. Ideally, the entire grouping should sit completely within an area rug. That means the smallest you can get away with for a conversation area is 5 x 8 feet—that's just large enough to accommodate a sofa and chair. Anything smaller ends up looking like a tiny island in the middle of your living room with a coffee table as its only inhabitant.

LEARN FROM VERN

LAYERING RUGS

Do you have a really special area rug that is simply too small to put in the center of a conversation area? Consider finding a solid color carpet that relates to one of the colors in your area rug and using that carpet as an anchor. Place the decorative rug strategically in the middle of the area rug, creating a wide border with the under rug, allowing the smaller rug to be admired as part of a rug ensemble.

CROWN MOLDING AND BASEBOARDS

Crown molding should never be higher than the baseboard in the same room. It is usually shorter or the same height. It seems logical that the base of something, whether it's a house or a tree trunk, should be the widest or biggest, since it's supporting the weight above it. For that reason, our eyes are accustomed to the base carrying more visual weight and thus being taller than the crown. In a room with 9- or 10-foot ceilings, for example, builder's grade 2-inch "clamshell" crown molding looks diminutive, like an afterthought. In a 1950s or 1960s modern home with 7-foot ceilings, crown molding tends to close the space in, aesthetically lowering the ceiling. In a room like this, you might be better off removing the crown and painting the walls and ceiling in a similar tone (with the ceiling slightly lighter) to create the effect of greater space.

If your crown and/or baseboard moldings are skimpy and you can't replace them (an often expensive process) deemphasize the deficiency by painting them the same color as the walls but in a gloss or semi-gloss finish if your wall paint is flat, eggshell, or satin. The difference in sheen creates a subtle nod to the crown and baseboard without drawing attention to their size. Likewise, if your ceilings are 8′-0″ or under, it's best to keep wall, trim, and ceiling as close in color to each other as possible. De-emphasizing the trim with paint is also generally considered a more contemporary approach to painting a room. It minimizes visual distractions in the room, creating a calmer feel overall.

TRIM BY THE NUMBERS

CROWN MOLDING, BASEBOARDS & WINDOW CASINGS

It may seem odd to talk about the proportions and dimensions of molding, which is often thought of as just being "there," attached to the walls in a room. On the other hand, "attached" is the operative word here. If molding is not working, it can be detached and replaced with something more appropriate. Trim in a room literally gives the space a frame, just as a picture frame does for a work of art. The right frame can make a painting or print stand out; the wrong one can minimize art or make it seem insignificant. Moldings in a room should elevate the space and make a room stand out, even if you're not really conscious of the trim all the time.

CROWN MOLDING

- **Less than 8′** Ceiling Height: Refrain if possible
- **8′** Ceiling Height: 3.0″ to 6.75″
- **9′** Ceiling Height: 4.0″ to 7.5″
- **10′** Ceiling Height: 5.0″ to 8.0″
- **12′** Ceiling Height: 7.0″ to10.0″

BASEBOARD HEIGHT

- **7′** Ceiling Height: 6.0″
- **8′** Ceiling Height: 6.75″ to 7.0″
- **9′** Ceiling Height: 7.5″ to 8.0″
- **10′** Ceiling Height: 8.0″ to 8.5″
- **12′** Ceiling Height: 10.0″ to 10.25″

DOOR AND WINDOW CASINGS

- These elements should not be wider than the baseboard height.
- For small to moderately sized rooms, and for rooms with numerous doors, windows, and/or wall openings, vertical trim should generally be no wider than 50 percent of the baseboard width. For example, in a standard room with 8' ceilings and 7-inch baseboards, your door and window casings should be no wider than 3.5 inches and your crown should be somewhere between 2.5 to 6.75 inches.

WAINSCOTING & CHAIR RAILS

Not every home can accommodate wainscoting and chair rails. Such embellishments are generally best left to spaces with ceiling heights of 9' or higher. Wainscoting and chair rails have the effect of visually diminishing the height of a wall by running horizontally across a wall plain and decreasing the sense of volume in a space. This diminishing effect is greater if the trim is painted in high contrast in relation to the wall color. If the color on the wall above and below the chair rail is not the same, then the color below a chair rail should always be darker than the color above. Doing the opposite may make you feel off balance; the foundation always should be weighted (think of how an inverted pyramid might make you feel).

WAINSCOTING

- **7'** Ceiling Height: Refrain if possible
- **8'** Ceiling Height: 32″
- **9'** Ceiling Height: 36″
- **10'** Ceiling Height: 40″
- **12'** Ceiling Height: 40″ to 48″

CHAIR RAILS

In general, a chair rail molding should section off the lower third of your wall space. That means measuring from 32 to 40 inches from the floor to the center of the molding you plan to use—depending on the height of your ceilings.

- **7'** Ceiling Height or Lower: Refrain if possible
- **8'** Ceiling Height: 32″ above finished floor
- **9'** Ceiling Height: 36″ above finished floor
- **10'** Ceiling Height or Higher: 40″ above finished floor. This may go higher if the chair rail is capping off wainscoting. Without wainscoting, a chair rail at this height doesn't generally make any sense.

OUTDOOR LIVING BY THE NUMBERS

SEATING AREAS

So many of us enjoy the out of doors; whether we have a city balcony or a big suburban backyard, we like living al fresco. There's no reason why outdoor living areas shouldn't be well designed, with the same attention to comfort and navigation that the interior of your home demands. Here are the numbers to know:

CALCULATION FOR MINIMUM SEATING AREAS

If you are building a patio, deck, courtyard, or any outdoor seating area, especially in a smaller space and want to be sure it's the right size for dining, use the following formula to determine the minimum amount of space you need for your chosen tables and chairs. If you have a large space and want to create multiple dining areas, simply use the result of your calculations for each area. It tells you just how much space you need for people to pull out chairs, sit down, and tuck themselves into the table:

Largest measurement of table (diameter or length) + half depth of the chair + whole depth of chair for backup + 12 to 18 inches for clearance. For an example, with a 48″ round table and 24″ deep chairs, you need: 48″ + 24″ + 12″ + 18″ = 102″ along that side.

FOUR SEATING AREA TYPES

There are four basic typical patio types; one of these should suit your space.

- **Bistro:** This is a great size for side yards, small yards in condos and town houses, or city balconies. These spaces are generally 6 to 7 feet in diameter, enough room to fit a table and two chairs, or two outdoor easy chairs and a drinks table. If you plan to lay flooring, consider using cobblestones or brick as opposed to large flagstone or pavers in a small space.

- **Living Room:** These popular multi-functional spaces should average at least 16 x 18 feet to accommodate guests and multiple functions. A good rule of thumb is to allow a 3-foot clearance around furniture. Larger pavers or flagstones can be used successfully in a space this expansive.

- **Outdoor Dining Room:** The minimum size to accommodate a 48-inch round table, which can seat 6 to 8 people depending on chair size, is a 13 foot x 13 foot square or round pad. This offers just enough space to pull out chairs, but not much walk around space. A 12- x 14-foot pad is the minimum pad size for a 72 inch rectangular table.

- **Lounging area:** A space for lounge chairs or sunning beds is a real perk in outdoor living spaces. To accommodate two to four 2 x 6-foot lounge chairs with small cocktail tables between them, plan for a 3-foot clear walking space past the foot of the chairs. Increase the minimum clearance around swimming pools from 3 feet to 5 feet to avoid unexpected dips in the pool.

WALKWAYS

Paths in a garden or outdoor space act as hallways and entry points to the various parts of your space. To encourage comfortable use, the paths should be wide enough for at least one person to navigate comfortably. However, how large you can make your path depends on the limits of space. Here are the typical measurements to walkable pathways:

- **24":** A bare minimum functional width, not ideal but serviceable if your space limitations give you no other choice.
- **30":** Functional for one person but not ideal.
- **36":** This is the standard width, and one I recommend.
- **48":** This is a wide path that accommodates two people side-by-side quite comfortably. A walkway this wide should be used in very large yards with expansive sightlines.

CHAPTER TWO: SHOP SMART

WHAT YOU NEED TO KNOW BEFORE YOU BUY

In the last chapter, we talked about proportion and size, the first considerations when designing timeless, livable rooms. Now let's turn our attention to what some consider the nitty-gritty of good design: the intrinsic qualities of each item you select for your home. We have an enormous number of furniture and accessory choices today, which is both wonderful and daunting. To help cut through the confusion that this abundance can create, I've put together a guide to what you need to know before you buy, whether it's in a home furnishing store, a flea market or auction, around the corner, or in a foreign land. This chapter helps you determine when and on what you should spend money and why.

Good-looking, functional, and personal design is absolutely within reach if you have access to basic principles. Whether you have a blank check to furnish your home or are on the tightest of budgets, keep in mind that furniture is an investment that should return value for many years to come. This is not to say that every item you buy for your home should be precious and valuable, or even brand-new, but everything should bring you joy, be well-made, attractive, and offer good value and function. Many years of designing on television, and having to purchase furniture with a limited budget, proved to me that quality can be affordable if you choose wisely. Beauty and function are achievable at every price point. Price is not an indication of or guarantee of quality. Just because something is expensive doesn't mean it's well-made, nor are inexpensive items necessarily poorly made. You can have a great-looking room for $1,000—start to finish—if you know what you're buying when choosing items to fill your space.

Buy things you love and you'll have them forever. While I was still in graduate school, I purchased a chair for $25 at an estate sale. It was the end of the day, after all the "good stuff" had already been bought. Except for my chair: it had very modern, aerodynamic lines. The legs were well made, and the frame was sturdy. I loved it. Eventually I had it reupholstered, and today it has a prominent place in my Manhattan apartment.

A classic pair of leather and chrome Corbusier chairs sits in the living room of my Atlanta house. I came upon them as an intern at my first job out of school, while helping in a remodel of an office building in downtown Atlanta. These iconic chairs had been in the building's lobby for 20 years, and the leather had some gentle and appealing wear, but overall they were in great shape. The owner of the office was selling them for $200 apiece. At the time that was a lot of money for me—I was barely getting by on $24,000 a year. Yet I knew what a great deal I would be getting. How could I let these chairs get away? I couldn't, so I got the cash together and ate Ramen noodles for a month. No regrets. Look for these kinds of opportunities because they do come along more often than you might think. You have to keep your eyes open and know what to look for in terms of quality, which is what this book can help you with. Seize the moment! Don't be afraid to ask salespeople and dealers questions. Get underneath a piece and examine it closely. Sit on or at it, try it out. Don't buy it unless you love it.

I also touch on identifying your personal aesthetic in this section. As you choose the finishes, furniture, and fixtures, you are making important style decisions. Design definitely goes through cycles and trends, and we have to be careful not to fall into a trend trap. For instance, when choosing fixtures for a bathroom or a kitchen, what sort of finish is going to stand the test of time? For a long time, brass fixtures, so popular in the 1970s and 1980s, were the first things to be removed from a kitchen or bath renovations during the early 2000s. Today, though, home and garden magazines proclaim that "brass is back," but not the lacquered style of the past—a more burnished finish is showing up in high-end design projects. But is it right for *you*? When you have a good grasp on your personal style, you can make informed decisions about when to follow—and when to ignore—a trend. Never embrace a trend unless you genuinely love it and it reflects your personal style.

When you shop, carry a tape measure, the dimensions of the room you are furnishing and accessorizing, and fabric swatches (if you have them). If you don't have access to fabric samples from your room, go to the paint department of your local hardware store and select paper paint swatches that closely approximate the colors in your space to use as color reference stand-ins. It doesn't hurt to bring along a photo of the room, either. Acquaint yourself with the numbers, features, and functions that make a purchase a worthy investment. Sometimes we buy an item because it's a "great deal," but is it really a bargain if it's the wrong size, color, or texture for your room? Avoid those mistakes by arming yourself with what you need to know, ask, and look for, when deciding between, for example, a 7-foot or a 9-foot sofa, or choosing materials, fabrics, and fixtures. The size and layout of your room determines how big you can go with major pieces, and where to put them in relation to other pieces in a room to create flow, harmony, and comfort.

WOOD FURNITURE:
IMPORTANT FACTS & FEATURES

You probably have a chair or table that belonged to Grandma, or maybe even Great-Grandmother. Chances are it was built to stand the test of time—and it has. Take a good look at it, and you'll probably see that it is solid, that its joints are still tight, and that, although softly glowing with the patina of time, it remains a totally functional piece. In this section, we'll discover why. Armed with this knowledge, you can make informed purchases of new furniture with the same durability.

While it's often true that "they don't build 'em like they used to," it's certainly also true that you can still buy good-quality wooden furniture that will also stand the test of time and the everyday wear-and-tear of family life. Be forewarned, however: there is a huge selection out there when shopping for wood furniture. And although it may seem that there is a stylish choice to fit every budget, purchasing a poorly made table or chair because the price is right may be an outright waste of your hard-earned money.

WOOD BASICS

Furniture made of wood can be constructed from solid wood, veneered solid wood or other material, or a manufactured product that may or may not include wood.

- **Solid Wood:** Wood furniture made with solid wood construction is often considered heartier and more durable because the visible wood is not just a surface material but runs through the structural components of the piece.

  Solid wood pieces can be sanded and refinished multiple times.

  There are two types of solid wood, hard and soft. Both are used in furniture, and either can be an option when you are furnishing your home, as long as you are aware of their differences.

- **Hardwood:** A hardwood comes from a deciduous tree, meaning a tree that loses its leaves seasonally, such as oak, maple, walnut, and cherry. In general, deciduous trees produce wood that's harder than that produced by softwood trees, but that's not always the case.

- **Softwood:** A softwood comes from a coniferous tree, which generally grows up more so than out. Coniferous trees bear cones and are mostly evergreen. One of the most popular softwoods to use in furniture is pine, which tends to be younger and softer than most hardwoods. Pine can often have knots that may affect the durability of furniture.

- **Real Wood Veneer:** Veneer is a very thin sheet of material—real wood with a beautiful grain, for example—that is affixed to the surface of a less attractive piece of solid wood or base material. When you look at a real wood veneered piece, the visible wood that you see is a wood skin that's been applied over a different solid wood, plywood, particle board, pressed wood, OSB (oriented strand board), MDF (medium-density fiberboard), or some other kind of underlying substrate. Real wood veneered furniture can be a showcase for some of the most beautiful woods there are. In the high-end furniture market, exotic, rare, or expensive species of wood are veneered on top of another kind of less costly wood. In the middle market, it is not unusual to find common wood species veneered on top of plywood. If that is the case, ensure that the plywood has a minimum of nine layers for stability and durability. Ask the salesperson if you cannot easily see the actual plywood and count the number of layers. A good salesperson should have access to the production details of the items in their showroom. In the lower end of the market, common wood species might be veneered on top of thin plywood, particleboard, pressed wood, OSB, or MDF. The durability of low-end pieces is not usually high, and you will likely have to replace these pieces in the not-too-distant future. While beauty is the appeal of real wood veneered furniture, it can be tricky to maintain. Look for the wood skin to be made of a wood that is resistant to scratching. The big disadvantage to real wood veneered pieces is that they either cannot be refinished or have limited refinishing capacities.

- **Imitation Wood Veneer:** Just because it looks like wood doesn't necessarily mean that it *is* wood. Oftentimes, the wood we see on low-end furniture is actually plastic laminate that has been veneered on top of thin plywood, particleboard, pressed wood, OSB, MDF, or another inexpensive substrate. The "wood" on these pieces won't have the luster and richness of real wood, and they will not be able to be sanded and re-finished. The structural core of these pieces also might not be as durable, so be prepared to replace these pieces after a potentially short or limited lifespan.

CONSTRUCTION DETAIL

After you've determined what type of wood you want your furniture piece to be, look next at how the piece has been constructed. Spend as much time studying the underside and insides of the piece before you buy. The visible wood surfaces are not the only important components to consider when analyzing furniture. Construction details can literally make or break a piece of furniture, and you need to know how to spot the good, the bad, and the ugly. One quick way to spot quality construction is to look for reinforcing blocks, triangular pieces placed in the corners where two structural pieces come together. These blocks help stabilize and brace the furniture, adding to the strength and lifespan of the furniture.

JOINTS

A great indicator of the quality of a wood furniture piece is the way that the individual components are joined together. Here is a breakdown of the most common joints in wooden furniture construction, in order of their strength, durability, and desirability. Again, keep in mind that initial expense can mean the difference between many years of use or another trip to the landfill after a few years. Always buy the best construction that you can afford.

- **Dovetail:** This is the gold standard of joints because of its resistance to being pulled apart. Two pieces come together with tails and pins that are trapezoidal in shape, interlocking and glued together to form a tight connection. There are various types of dovetail joints, but they're all generally considered durable and a sign of solid construction.

- **Mortise and Tenon:** Another high-quality wood furniture joint, because of its strength. In its simplest form, a mortise is a specifically sized square or rectangular hole designed for the tenon tongue to fit exactly. Most modern furniture pieces employing mortise and tenon joints also use glue to ensure that the pieces lock securely into place.

- **Dowels:** Dowels are round wooden pins that insert into pre-drilled holes on both sides of the wood components that are being joined together. Glue is usually applied to both ends of the dowels to ensure that they remain in place.

- **Biscuit:** In this joint type, a crescent-shaped slot is made in the two pieces being joined by a biscuit joiner. A thin, oval-shaped wooden biscuit is then covered in glue and inserted into the slots to hold the two wood pieces together. It's not generally considered as strong as other forms of joinery, but it's also not as common.

- **Butt:** By merely butting two straight pieces of wood together and then attaching them with screws, nails, and/or staples form a butt joint, as the name implies. Glue is used in almost all types of joints as an additional element to help hold them together. However, butt joints that depend on glue alone, glue and staples, or glue and nails only could be weak and prone to failure.

DRAWERS

Drawers are a great way to organize your home, so it's important to understand what makes a quality one that will operate long term.

- **Glides and Stops:** If you're looking for high-functioning drawers that allow plenty of easy, accessible storage, consider a modern-day piece over an antique one. Quality modern-day wooden furniture generally has drawers on metal glides that facilitate smooth opening and closing. They should also have stops that prevent the drawers from being pulled completely out. Most high-quality antique pieces, on the other hand, do not have metal glides or stops, although they might have wooden rails to help keep the drawers on track when opening and closing, but they don't operate in a comparable manner.

- **Bottoms:** Look for solid wood or multi-layered plywood bottoms that will stand the test of time. OSB (oriented strand board), particleboard, MDF (medium density fiberboard), and other inferior materials will likely give or warp after years of normal to heavy use. Quality drawers also have bottoms that float inside grooves that run along the sides of a drawer instead of being affixed to the drawer sides. By floating within these grooves, the wooden drawer can expand and contract with changes in humidity and temperature without affecting function.

- **Dust Panels:** Thin sheets of wood that separate drawers, protecting the contents from getting dust on them while adding to the overall structural integrity. Although they're a nice added feature to have, they aren't absolutely necessary.

LEARN FROM VERN

CONSTRUCTION

My preference is to buy solid wood construction or real wood veneer over another solid wood or thick (9-layer or more) plywood substrate. A salesperson should be able to give you all the construction specifications of a new piece of furniture. This information may be more difficult to discern when buying an older piece or an antique. However, many older pieces of furniture were well made. Check the sturdiness of the structure before you buy and always ask the dealer about the history of the piece. It may cost more upfront, but you will save in the long run with furniture that will last as long as you need it to and perhaps long enough to pass on to your children. It's also less damaging to the environment, since you are not filling our landfills with discarded "temporary" furniture.

WOOD KNOTS

When looking at wood furniture, whether hardwood or softwood, look for "clean" surfaces that are free from knots and other imperfections that may impact the structural performance of the wood. The knot is an area that can be susceptible to cracking and will expand and contract differently than other parts of the wood surface. This is also true for any plywood substrate that lies below a wood veneer. Even if the wood veneer itself looks good, if the plywood has knots in it, the structural integrity of the piece may be compromised.

UPHOLSTERED FURNITURE:
IMPORTANT FACTS & FEATURES

The kitchen may be the "heart of the home," but let's face it, we use our living and family spaces for entertaining, hanging out, watching television, or listening to music—and often consuming the goodies that come out of the kitchen. The "heart" notwithstanding, our formal and informal living spaces tend to have the most furniture *and* the most expensive furniture and accessories. Sofa or sectionals and other upholstered furniture represent a major purchase; however, not all upholstery is created equal.

When you go shopping, bring my handy guidelines and cheat sheets (pages 276–282) with you. Then, find a knowledgeable salesperson and ask them questions about how the pieces you're interested in are made, using what follows as a guide. A good salesperson should be able to answer any question you throw at them. If you're looking online, call the 800-number and speak to an associate about things you're interested in. If you don't get satisfactory answers, move on.

Here are the basic qualities of all upholstered furniture, including sofas, sectionals, arm and lounge chairs, as well as chaises and upholstered benches, you should discuss with your furniture dealer *before* you plunk your credit card down:

- **Ask about the frame.** Your first consideration when purchasing upholstered seating should be its construction—the parts you never see.
  - » Soft wood frames, such as those made from pine, are low-cost, but can warp after just five years of daily use.
  - » Hardwood frames like kiln-dried oak, ash, or beech are much stronger, and can last many decades or more.
  - » Stay away from frames made of particleboard, plastic, or metal; they may warp and crack.
- **Legs** should be part of the frame or held on with screws or dowels (pegs) – not with glue alone.
- **Springs**. Look for "eight-way hand-tied springs," a symbol of quality in the furniture industry. This method uses long lasting coil springs tied together in eight directions with twine, which provides stability and comfort.

RAPHAEL
TITIAN

- **Don't forget cushion composition.** What's inside cushions is really important because a lot of inexpensive sofas will have low-density foam cushions. This type of foam insert may feel comfortable when you sit on the piece in the showroom. After a few months into owning the piece, your favorite part of the sofa will be clear to everyone because the foam starts to break down and condense as people consistently sit in the same spot. Even if you want a soft seat, you want it to last.

  » High-density foam cushion wrapped in down gives you great bounce back and shape. That means you're not adjusting the cushion every time you get up, but it is comfortable and soft. Low- or standard-density foam is probably never going to be what you want it to be.

  » Super fluffy, plush cushions that are 100% feather- or down-stuffed are found on some high-end sofas and chairs; they are comfy but high-maintenance. Every time you get up, the seat looks lumpy. You either live with that look, or go to the extra effort to fluff up the cushion every time you get up.

  » Very firm, unwrapped high-density foam is not as soft as high-density foam wrapped in down or fiberfill. This might be a better choice for upholstered benches, or other upholstered surfaces that are not sat on for long periods of time or for those who like an extremely firm seat.

- **Are the cushions reversible?** Even medium grade sofas don't always have this wonderful feature that allows the seat cushions to be flipped because the top and bottom of the cushion are covered in the same fabric. A reversible cushion is a genuine benefit and extends the life of your sofa; don't take it for granted. The same is true for reversible loose back chair and couch cushions.

- **Fabric composition is crucial.** Of course you should focus on the color, pattern, and texture of the upholstery you choose. However, the fabric itself impacts performance, function, and ease of cleaning.

  » Many people spend money upholstering chairs and sofas in linen and silk. These are beautiful fabrics, but they are not especially durable and can require special care to clean. Generally, these fabrics should be reserved for elegant furniture that will not be the subject of daily use, and the wear and tear that goes with it. Pure linen wrinkles easily, so be prepared to live with that look if you choose this fabric.

  » Look for a polyester blend if you want durability and affordability. That can mean a cotton/poly blend, a linen/poly blend, or even a wool/poly blend. Polyester makes all of these natural fabrics more durable, as well as fade and wrinkle resistant. In general, they are more affordable than "100%" fabrics, and textile technology has advanced so much that, these days, it's hard to tell a poly blend from a non-blend.

  » Mohair is a great fabric in terms of quality. However, it's very expensive. In this case, you truly get what you pay for. Mohair is beautiful, soft, luxurious, resilient, and comfortable.

  » Leather is a good material for upholstered seating if you have kids, if you want something that is very durable and resistant to staining, and is wipeable. There are many different kinds of leather. Very smooth and refined leather is susceptible to scratching, however over time that wear can add to a lovely, warm patina. Distressed leather doesn't show as much damage because it's already been treated to have a well-worn look. Avoid "bonded leather"–in some cases it is not even leather and if it is, it is low-grade leather made from leftover, processed remnants.

SECTIONAL SMARTS

Sectionals are widely popular today and can be found in a wide variety of sizes and configurations. When purchasing a sectional, ask the same questions regarding the manufacturing and composition of the sectional recommended for sofas and lounge chairs.

In my experience, it is very difficult to design a timeless room that is both functional and aesthetically pleasing when a sectional, particularly a generous one, is part of the picture. Sectionals dominate any room they are in, and effectively divide the room wherever they are placed, much like a wall would. Unless you have a cavernous space, it's hard to get around this.

Most folks think having a sectional is a great solution if you need to accommodate a lot of people in one room. I don't necessarily agree. There are very few people I've come across who want to sit in the corner of a sectional, since there is no leg room to speak of. This corner, in my opinion, is not a great use of precious space in most rooms. I'd rather have two sofas coming together with the corner occupied by a drink or accessory table that would at least provide a needed function. However, if you're determined to include a sectional in your room, here are some critical factors to keep in mind:

- **Space plan.** Make sure that you still have plenty of room for passage, and that you can also accommodate a coffee table and side tables comfortably.
- **Be height smart.** Try to avoid sectionals with backs taller than 38 inches. When you have a single piece of furniture that is this massive and dominant, having a high back increases the visual mass even more so.
- **Keep it casual.** Sectionals convey a casual quality, so it's best to limit their use to massive rooms that you want to have this feel.
- **Double-check.** Before finalizing a decision to purchase a sectional, ask yourself one last time if you can't accomplish the same accommodation of people and comfort with a grouping of sofas, love seats, chaise lounges, lounge chairs, ottomans, and daybeds. If you can, you'll at least have the flexibility to move these pieces around into different spaces in the future if you should move. Sectionals can also be broken up into smaller pieces, but you often have awkward corner pieces and end pieces with no matching mate on the other side.

LEARN FROM VERN

HAVE A SEAT

It's always best to try a sofa out for yourself, in person, to ensure that it suits you and it's comfortable. If that's not possible, such as when you are ordering online, or if you're researching online first before deciding which models are worthy of an in-person visit, add the seat height to the seat depth to see if you end up somewhere between 40 to 44 inches. Shorter individuals are generally more comfortable with a combined measurement of 40 inches, whereas taller individuals are usually more comfortable closer to the 44-inch combined measurement. Nothing, of course, beats trying it out in person, since we're all proportioned differently.

THINK BEYOND THE SOFA

You may want to forego a living room sofa entirely and opt instead for two chairs, a lounge, or a daybed instead. It's a versatile look I've used successfully in many rooms. Good quality alternatives are available at lower cost than sofas, and also bring with them the added benefit of solving some of the design dilemmas posed by a sofa. When looking into the backs of two chairs rather than one sofa, for instance, you're greeted by a much less daunting and singular mass. Consider what your chair backs look like, and perhaps select something with an interesting frame or line. A backless daybed or lounge opens up the visuals in the room by removing the height of a back the sofa would necessitate.

FLIPPING OUT

It doesn't take a great deal of effort to maintain your furniture, but it is so worth it in terms of extending their life. I take the inserts out of my seat cushions and flip them, like a mattress, and reinsert them once a year. If you don't do this, over time the front edge of the seat cushion slopes and gets worn. The same is true of rugs. Once a year they should be flipped so wear patterns do not become an obvious trail across a beautiful carpet. When you do this, you expand the chance of having great furnishings for more years than you expect.

DINING FURNITURE:
IMPORTANT FACTS & FEATURES

While it's easy to agree on the purpose of a dining room—family meals, entertaining friends, socializing with the boss—all bets are off when it comes to agreeing on how it should be furnished. What shape should the table be? Should it be a conventional height or the taller "gathering table" currently in fashion? What size fits what number of people? And that's just the table—the chairs pose their own set of choices and challenges. Here are straightforward guidelines to help you make the right decision.

TABLETOPS

The most common shapes for dining room tabletops are rectangular, round, and oval. Rectangles are perhaps the most common because they are space-efficient and better suited to the proportions of typical dining rooms. The major drawback to rectangular tables is the inability to easily converse or interact with all diners at the table, especially at tables longer than 72 inches. Round tables work best for rooms with proportions closer to a square, and they are great for facilitating conversation, since each person is visible to every other person. Keep in mind, though, that round tables may take up more floor space than rectangular tables to seat the same number of people.

TABLE BASES

There is a wide variety of dining table bases but most can be categorized into one of three main types, with each style impacting the number and placement of chairs the table can comfortably accommodate.

- **Pedestal:** This base supports the table from the center and can be the most adaptable style when seating flexibility is important. Round tables typically have only one pedestal, whereas rectangular and oval tables may have one or more pedestals.
- **Corner Legs:** The most restrictive of base styles, legs placed at the four corners of a rectangular table or placed equidistant on a round table dictate chair placement with little flexibility.
- **Trestle, or Stretcher:** This style features a stretcher that runs the length of the table and is attached to an inset support placed several feet from each end. A trestle table offers more flexible seating than a corner-leg style, but often less than a pedestal base. Make sure that the inset supports don't interfere with chair placement.

DINING CHAIRS

- **Upholstered vs. non-upholstered:** Don't assume that, because a dining chair is upholstered, it will be comfortable. Most upholstered dining chairs do not have spring beds, which afford great support and bounce. An upholstered dining seat is often much thinner than that of a standard upholstered chair. You won't know until you sit down. Wood, leather, woven, or other forms of chair seats may be more durable and easier to keep clean.
- **Arms or no arms:** Arms take up space and create awkward right angles around a circular table, so armless chairs may fit more comfortably in this instance. However, at a rectangular table, you might want to look for two armchairs for each end of the table, and use armless chairs down each side of the table. Mix up the styles of chairs for more visual interest.

ACCESSORY FURNITURE:
IMPORTANT FACTS & FEATURES

STOOLS

Stools are both classic and part of a trend in household furnishings. The trend itself—pub tables and so-called "gathering" tables—is a fading flash in the pan, and we'll soon be seeing these silly, impractical sets go the way of "authentic Tuscan" kitchens. However, stools on their own are compact, fit well into most any kitchen design that includes a counter bar or island, and are comfortable. Here's what to look for when purchasing bar stools for your home:

- **Round stools.** These seats take up a little less space than square ones of comparable size. If you are tight on space, consider a round stool over a square one.
- **Backless stools.** A great choice for use in the middle of a room, since they can be sat on facing the counter/table or away from it without physically turning the stool itself. They're also less disruptive to the flow of a room.
- **Stool swivel seats.** Wonderful for versatility and comfort in tight or restrictive spaces. They are also smart choices when stools are in the middle of a room, since the seat can easily be turned to address either side of the space it is located in.
- **Sized for comfort.** Small children, petite adults, and adults who frequently wear fitted skirts and/or very high heels may find bar and spectator-height or extra tall stools (34 to 36 inches to the seat) a little more challenging to get into than table-height or counter-height stools. A properly placed foot rung or support can help. If you or one of your family members may have a problem getting in and out of a stool, make sure to try it out in the store first with the restrictive elements in place to ensure that it won't become a problem at home.
- **Stools with backs.** The best choice when they're going to be used frequently for long periods–at mealtime, for example, or at homework time. The extra support provided by a back generally makes it more comfortable in the long run. There are also stool options that offer both a back and a swivel seat for enhanced comfort and versatility.
- **Adjustable seats.** For households with small kids, consider stools with adjustable seats and extra stability. Also, consider stools that can be easily wiped or cleaned. Metal, polycarbonate, smooth leather, and other easily cleaned materials can be especially good choices if eating, coloring, or creating crafts at these stools will occur. Avoid woven seats that can trap food particles and delicate upholstery that might stain easily.
- **Arm yourself.** Measure the clear distance from the finished floor to the underside of the table or countertop if you are considering a stool with arms to ensure that those arms can be tucked below the surface level. Arms that cannot be tucked underneath will cause the stool to take up significantly more space and may make it less accessible to the table or counter.
- **Aesthetics matter.** Choose a stool that fits into the overall balance of your room. Be careful to not pick stools that are overtly ornate if your kitchen cabinet style or countertop design is already aesthetically very busy. If your kitchen cabinets and countertops are fairly simple and understated, a more ornate stool can have the necessary room to breathe and become a major focal point.
- **Counter style.** Stools at a kitchen counter don't need to match adjacent dining chairs. In fact, it is probably best if they do not. Choose a style that is distinct but complementary. Consider a common finish or metal color as the common thread to tie the seating elements together.

BENCHES

Benches are versatile pieces that can be used for so many different purposes. In an entryway or at the end of a bed, they provide a good place to sit down and take off or put on shoes. I've used them as a coffee table in between two facing sofas in a narrow room, and even as extra seating in a living room. Depending on the seat height, a bench can also be a good seating option for a dining room table. When placed in front of a nice view, it becomes an instant "window seat" without the construction. Here's what to keep in mind when shopping for a bench.

- **Width matters.** Most benches are between 18 to 20 inches tall, but the width can vary. To comfortably seat two people, look for a bench that is at least 48 inches wide.
- **Scale it.** A bench placed at the foot of a bed should be at least 4 inches narrower than the bed itself. For instance, if your queen-size bed is 60 inches wide, your bench should be no more than 56 inches wide. Anything bigger looks awkward.
- **Check quality.** To ensure the bench is well made, flip it over and check to see how the legs are attached to the seat frame. Legs and base should be solidly joined together with no spaces between parts. If the bench has fasteners, they should be screws, which are much more stable than nails or staples.
- **Tone and finish.** A backless wood bench is a great staple and versatile. It doesn't have to match all the other wood in a room, but it should be in a similar tone and finish.
- **Soft spot.** If you do use a backless bench at your dining room table, consider adding a cushion if a softer feel is needed for longer meals, or use an upholstered bench.

  An upholstered bench will show wear, just like any other upholstered piece. Choose a durable fabric. An indoor/outdoor fabric is extremely sturdy and both stain- and water-resistant. Plus, indoor/outdoor fabric now comes in a huge array of colors and textures, making it easier than ever to find something that works with your décor.

COFFEE & ACCESSORY TABLES:
IMPORTANT FACTS & FEATURES

Finding the perfect coffee table for your room can sometimes be a daunting process. Again, you can succeed if you begin with some basic planning. In Chapter One, we looked at the dimensions of the piece you are looking for, but let's review them again. Remember, coffee table lengths should never exceed sofa lengths. For ease, here are ideal coffee table lengths for most standard length sofas. Note that once you go beyond a 72-inch sofa, a round table will be difficult to accommodate seamlessly into your seating arrangement, since it will likely be smaller than two-thirds of your overall sofa length.

- **72" sofa:** 48" coffee table length, or 36" to 48" diameter for a round table
- **84" sofa:** 56" coffee table length
- **96" sofa:** 64" coffee table length
- **108" sofa:** 72" coffee table length
- **120" sofa:** 80" coffee table length

Next, determine the shape and the material of the table that best meets your functional and aesthetic needs.

SHAPE

Shape is critical to making sure that your pairing is both functional and aesthetically pleasing. Space-plan your room first to help determine the best shape and optimal size for your room. Here are the most common shapes:

- **Rectangle:** The majority of coffee table options are rectangles, since most rooms are proportioned to best accommodate this shape. If you already have round side tables or a sofa with rolled arms or a camel back, a rectangular coffee table offers nice counter balance. Too many right angles or too many curves in one room can aesthetically visually throw off the room's balance.
- **Oval:** In almost any situation where a rectangle will fit, an oval will fit, too. The added advantage with an oval is that it's slightly easier to get around and doesn't have the sharp angles that kids sometime injure themselves on. For narrow rooms where providing enough space to traverse around a coffee table is problematic, this can be a good option. The disadvantage is that (when compared to similarly sized rectangles) they tend to have less surface area for placing items on. For rooms with plenty of right angles, an oval can provide needed softness and relief. If you have a lot of curves on your seating choice, an oval table may not be the ideal choice.
- **Square:** These surfaces offer plenty of tabletop for rooms that can accommodate them and can be grouped to form extra-large rectangular tables, which can be difficult to find. Small squares are also good for grouping in situations where the flexibility of breaking them apart is more attractive than having a single rectangle, or where it proportionally makes more sense than available rectangular options.
- **Round:** Equally accessible from all sides, a round coffee table is a welcoming shape when placed in the middle of a conversation pit; however, rooms should be generous to accommodate round tables, since they normally have diameters of 36 to 42 inches, and they can be challenging to place in front of sofas longer than 72 inches. Since most upholstery is square or rectangular in shape, a round coffee table can provide that needed visual relief from all of those right angles. Their lack of sharp corners makes them more kid-friendly than rectangles or squares. Seek out a taller round table (20 to 21 inches in height) with a cleanable top to use as an eating table or activities table for young kids whose seats typically have a height of 12 to 13 inches from the finished floor. When they've outgrown sitting around it, it can easily convert back to a coffee table function. With less surface area than a comparably sized rectangular coffee table, round tables will have a little less usable and accessible surface area, so make sure that's not a priority for you before you consider one.

THE HISTORY
OF SURFING
MATT WARSHAW

MATERIAL

Coffee tables are available in a dizzying array of materials. When picking one, consider the style and material of your sofa, and select your table to balance out the overall combination.

- **Lacquered or Painted:** If you want your coffee table to be the center of attention rather than a supporting player, consider a lacquered or painted example in a bright, bold, or saturated color. Keep in mind that not every item in a room can or should provide a "look at me" moment, so decide where you'd like your eye to focus before embracing bold color everywhere. Paired with neutral upholstery or in a predominantly neutral space, a colorful coffee table can be great way to enliven a space.

- **Glass or Acrylic:** These materials are great choices for small rooms that can benefit from less visual obstruction. They're also good choices if you have a great rug pattern that you'd like to be more visible. Glass is ideal for coffee tables that see plenty of entertaining with food and drinks, since their surfaces are easy to wipe or clean. If you're thinking about an acrylic or Lucite coffee table, remember that this material is fairly susceptible to scratching. For large rooms that need to up the cozy factor, these clear materials may not be a great choice, since they don't do much for grounding a room.

- **Metal:** Coffee table designs in this material cover a wide style range, from über-traditional to space age contemporary. Metal finishes come in everything from bright golds to polished chromes and rustic bronzes. Polished metal is a great choice for rooms that lack natural light, since they tend to brighten a room by bouncing that natural light back into the space. In general, metal coffee tables tend to be more open and leggy due to the nature of the material. They're a great counterpoint to rooms that are already dominated by a lot of wood and are a nice relief from a sea of upholstery. For rooms that already have a lot of metal side tables, lighting, accessories, and upholstery with metal detailing such as nail heads, look to other materials, such as wood, to warm and ground the space.

- **Stone:** All-stone coffee tables are hard to find. However, stone-topped coffee tables are common, and when properly sealed, a great alternative to glass if you're looking for a durable surface from which to serve food and drinks. Depending on the type and color, stone can be warm and welcoming or cool and austere, so choose carefully. If you already have a lot of stone in your space in the form of floors, fireplaces, and other tables, avoid a stone coffee table top and look to another material to either lighten or warm things up. If you have wood floors and a wood fireplace mantle, a stone coffee table top can be an element that adds visual interest and texture to a room. As with countertops, be cautious if you're looking at a soft stone top like white marble or limestone, as these materials stain more easily than harder surfaces like granite or quartz (check my guide to countertops on page 31). Natural stone tops need to be re-sealed every so often to ensure that their porous surfaces don't hold water marks and other stains.

- **Wood:** One of the most widely available materials when looking at coffee tables, wood can be durable, warm, and welcoming. For sleek sofas up on metal legs, a wood coffee table could be the perfect companion to help warm things up. If your sofa has exposed wood detailing, or the room your coffee table is going in already has a lot of wood, consider a brighter and different material, such as polished metal or glass, to help alleviate any potential heaviness. Remember, too, that a wooden tabletop must be protected from inevitable food and beverage spills.

STORAGE

The coffee table is an essential piece of furniture because of its versatility. And versatility means one size need not fit all. You can put your coffee table to work by having it do double duty as a storage unit. And you can be flexible in your definition of what constitutes a coffee table.

Most homes lack enough storage, no matter how big they are or how many closets are in them. Although an airy, open, and leggy coffee table can be elegant and a needed counterpoint to bulky upholstery pieces, they're not great options if you have storage issues. A coffee table can be a wonderful source of needed storage rather than just a place to serve guests dessert or display beautiful coffee table books. Here are some ways coffee tables can afford you useful storage:

- **Shelves:** Even one shelf integrated into a coffee table can prove useful. If the shelf allows for it, organizing devices like baskets can sit on a coffee table shelf to store items you want accessible but don't normally want to see, such as remote controls.

- **Drawers:** These are harder to find in a coffee table but an excellent place to store a remote, coasters, and other small but useful items. Because items behind drawers can't be seen, it's easy and practical storage as long as your items are scaled to fit.

- **Doors:** Great for storing larger and bulkier items that won't normally fit into a drawer, such as a large blanket you use to cozy up on the couch with, board games, and children's toys. Look for opaque doors versus ones with glass to keep your mess out of sight.

- **In-Body:** Occasionally, you can find a coffee table with a top that lifts up, revealing a big and open cavity within. This is great option if toys or craft items overrun your house. It can also be a great place to store items you bring out for entertaining, such as large trays, linens, etc. If your sofa doubles as a sofa bed, it's an ideal place for the accompanying bedding. If you use it for toy storage, just make sure that it's being opened and closed by an adult or that there is some kind of working safety mechanism in place to prevent the possibility of injuries when kids access their items.

LEARN FROM VERN

MATCHING SEATING TO TABLE

It's important to stylistically balance a sofa and coffee table pairing, since they're typically in direct adjacency to each other. Chunky and large-scaled sofas with almost no visible feet often look best paired with leggy coffee tables. Conversely, leggy and streamlined sofas look best paired with a coffee table that possesses a little mass. Consider detailing as well: A sofa with an intricately carved frame or one that sports a busy pattern needs the visual relief provided by a clean-lined and simple coffee table. A very plain and unadorned sofa benefits from a coffee table that features an unusual shape, extra detailing, or one made from an interesting material, like an exotic wood, or that has an unusual texture.

BOOK SMART

I love decorating with books. They are colorful and architectural, not to mention informative. Lavishly illustrated "coffee table books" are not the only kind of volumes that personalize a space. Remove the covers of your favorite novels, nonfiction, or books of poetry (store them carefully) and stack the books neatly for a graphic effect and a pop of color. Consider stacking like-color or complimentary colored bindings together. While enjoying the design appeal of this strategy, your guests can also gather insight into your reading preferences—and may enjoy dipping into your collection as they relax.

ALTERNATIVES

If a conventional coffee table won't work for you, or if you just want to do something unconventional, consider one of the following options:

- **Ottomans:** This is wonderful, casual option if you like to prop your feet up on a coffee table or need the flexibility of extra seating. It's also a wonderful option if you have kids, since the soft corners really help prevent injuries. Many ottomans even provide storage within their bodies, making them ideal for family rooms overrun by toys. If you have kids, dogs, a messy family, or like to prop your feet up with shoes on, consider a durable leather option.

- **Multiple Tables:** Since side tables are both (more often than not) taller and narrower than typical coffee tables, grouping them to form a larger surface is a great option if you regularly eat at your coffee table or use it for entertaining purposes. Higher side tables as coffee tables are also great for folks who like to place their laptops on them. Keep a side table grouping in front of a sofa no more than 2 to 3 inches above the seat height to prevent it from both looking odd and being too difficult to employ for more typical uses.

  » Butting two or more identical coffee table or ottoman units together to create one larger unit substantial enough to reach your adjacent seating areas.

  » Establish a secondary coffee table designed to address a secondary seating area. Sometimes it's just not practical to find or have a single massive coffee table in the middle of your seating area space. Create a smaller secondary coffee table with a table or grouping of tables that are visually linked to your primary coffee table by material or color to help tie it all together.

- **Garden Stools:** Both great as side tables, extra seating, and grouped as an impromptu coffee table, these have the added benefit of typically being made of an easy to clean surface like ceramic or porcelain. With standard heights in the range of 16 to 18 inches, they're perfect as a secondary coffee table or for smaller spaces where storage is not an issue but flexibility and extra seating is.

- **Benches:** Great for extremely narrow spaces where you'd still like to have a coffee table and need more continuous surface area than a few grouped side tables or garden stools would provide. Seek out a bench with a lower seat (unless you need the extra height), since most have seat heights closer to 18 to 19 inches rather than the typical 15 to 18 inches needed for a coffee table. Most won't have any built-in storage capability but come with the added benefit of easy conversion to extra seating.

BEDROOM FURNITURE:
IMPORTANT FACTS & FEATURES

Do cast your design net beyond the matching pieces of a "bedroom set" when shopping for bedroom furniture. You can create a richer and more interesting look that will endure the test of time if you search out complementary pieces that combine in a harmonious whole. If your existing bedroom furniture is made of heavy, solid wood, for example, consider an upholstered or polished metal bed. Here are some other points to keep in mind:

- **Bed Selection:** Beds are often one of the single largest pieces of furniture in your entire house, especially if you're sleeping in a king or California king. Almost certainly, they're the biggest statement piece in a bedroom. Select your bed style carefully because it will set the tone for the rest of your bedroom. When making your selection, assess the entire bedroom furniture situation. If you have existing bedroom furniture you'll be working with, your bed selection will need to balance out what you already have. If your bed is the first thing you'll be purchasing, it will greatly impact the shape and materials of the other components you'll be adding afterward.

- **Balancing Detail:** No matter what your style, it's important to balance the level of detail in your bedroom. A bedroom filled with detailed furniture and artifacts can benefit from a simple and clean-lined bed. If you've got a lot of upholstered seating in the bedroom, consider a more structured bed in wood. A bedroom outfitted with stark furniture and accessories benefits from a bed with some detailing, texture, or intricacy. If you've got a lot of hard, orthogonal edges (squares and rectangles), for instance, consider a headboard that sports some curves. Conversely, if you've got round nightstands and sloped arms on your upholstery, balance your room out with a bed that has clean and sharp angles.

- **Balancing Tones:** Rather than purchasing your nightstands, dressers, and bed in one color, mix things up in related tones so that they feel purposeful while still exhibiting individual interest. If you're purchasing several items in wood, for example, pick different but related wood tones with similar undertones. Oftentimes, if you look at wood carefully, you'll see a multitude of subtle color variations in the graining that you can then easily pull from. Metal hardware on wood nightstands is a great entry point for picking a metal bed in a different finish but within the same metal family. By mixing colors of woods, metals, and fabrics, you can create a layered and satisfying look that will endure.

BEDS

Generally speaking, every style of bed on the following list comes in sizes to accommodate the standard U.S. mattress sizes below. Take careful measurements when purchasing an antique bed, since many antique bed frames were not designed to accommodate modern-day U.S. mattress sizes.

- **Placement:** In general, it's best to place a bed against a logical, solid wall; one that faces the best view or a television, if you enjoy nighttime viewing. If that's not possible, and the best location happens to be against a window, make sure you're able to see through the headboard of your bed. An "open" style headboard allows the light and view in.

- **Platform:** This style of bed is closest to the ground and is often employed in more contemporary bedrooms. Most commonly used without a box spring, platform-style beds typically sit about 17 to 18 inches from finished floor to the top of the mattress. If you are in a tight bedroom situation with no room for a bench or chair, the mattress height on a platform bed is somewhere between sofa height and standard dining chair height—so it can be convenient for sitting on the edge comfortably.

- **Headboard only:** Sticking with just a headboard is a great choice any time space is an issue. There are a wide variety of both upholstered and hard surface headboard styles that can easily attach to an inexpensive metal frame.

- **Headboard, Side Rails, and Foot Rail:** This style of bed usually requires a little more room than just a headboard, making it a good option for standard- to smaller-sized bedrooms. The side rails and foot or end rail sit below the mattress top.

- **Headboard, Side Rails, and Footboard:** A headboard and footboard that extend above the height of the mattress create a more formal look, and are best used in average-to-generous bedrooms where passage space is not an issue. For example, the sleigh bed, which has curved headboards and footboards, definitely requires a decent amount of space.

- **Four Poster:** Similar to a bed frame with a headboard and footboard, this style of bed has extended posts on all four corners to create vertical drama and is generally employed in more traditional or transitional settings.

- **Canopy:** With rods or rails connecting the posts extending from the four corners of the bed, this style almost creates a bedroom within a bedroom. Decorative or functional sheers or fabric panels can be hung from these rods or rails to add extra visual softness to a space or close off the bed to the rest of the bedroom.

DOUBLE-DUTY BEDS

Your bed can be a great source of storage if you put some forethought into it. Here are some ways to accomplish that:

- **Storage Below the Bed:** Beds up on legs offer an opportunity to use the space under the bed for storage. Purchase lidded containers that fit below the bed to house seasonal bedding not in use, excess clothing, or other items that need to be protected from the dust that normally gathers in this spot. Depending on how tall your bed legs are, you may need a bed skirt to hide all the storage below.
- **Storage Drawers:** Some beds have built-in drawers in their platforms. This is a great way to easily store items in a clean environment, as long as you don't mind seeing the drawers from the side of the bed. Make sure that those drawers can still be accessed even with nightstands in place.
- **Storage Headboards:** Although not as popular today, some manufacturers offer headboards with built in shelving accessed from the side or from the front. These headboards are usually deeper because of this storage feature, so they may not be a great choice for small bedrooms.
- **Storage Built into the Bed:** These types of beds are not as prevalent as the other options I've listed, but there are manufacturers who've supplanted the space normally taken up by box springs with storage accessed by lifting up the mattress platform. This is a great way to gain clean, compartmentalized storage that you may desperately need if you're living in tight quarters. Depending on the size of your bed, it could be the equivalent of gaining an entire linen closet without taking up valuable additional square footage.

NIGHTSTANDS

There is room in even the most diminutive bedroom for its second-most indispensable piece of furniture, the nightstand. Whether it's a place for your eyeglasses, or a spot for your evening milk and cookies, a small table adjacent to your bed is a must-have for most of us. A nightstand should have some amount of storage, even if it's just a single drawer or shelf. Even the minimalist who doesn't read, watch TV, or bring water to bed will usually find having one built-in storage component in a nightstand helpful.

For a nightstand to functional optimally, you should first know the measurement of the top of your mattress from the finished floor. Your nightstands should then be within approximately 2 inches (shorter or taller) of this measurement. This allows easy access to lamps, water, books, phones, or anything else you may need to easily reach from bed.

- **Nightstands:** These tables should not be deeper than 25 inches to allow you easy in-and-out access to your bed without banging into it.
- **Alternatives:** The perfect "nightstand" might not actually be intended as a nightstand. Dressers, desks, buffets, side tables, accent tables, vanities, small entry tables, and low bookcases are all viable options to use as nightstands, as long as they're not deeper than 25 inches and within 2 inches of the height of the mattress from the finished floor. For smaller apartments and homes, having multi-functional nightstands is a fantastic way to save space and add storage.
- **Looks matter:** Your nightstands sit right next to your bed, so it's important that they work with your bed aesthetically. Look for nightstands that relate to your bed without feeling like they were extruded from the same factory. Here are a few ways to do that:
  - Avoid having too many blocky or leggy items in a row. If your bed is very solid in appearance, seek out nightstands with legs. If your bed is more delicate and up on legs, balance this out with nightstands that are more grounded and blocky in appearance.
  - Opposites can bring out the best in each other. Choose materials that complement each other without being redundant. A metal bed pairs wonderfully with wood nightstands. Similarly, a wood bed looks smart juxtaposed to mirrored or metal nightstands. A fabric headboard looks great sitting next to almost anything, as long as it's not also upholstered.

- **Form meets function:** Nightstands need to be the perfect confluence of function and aesthetics, and more importantly, tailored to the user's needs. If they don't function properly, you'll be unhappy with them, no matter how great they look. It's important to take into consideration habits such as bringing a glass of water to bed each night, reading at bedtime, or grabbing an extra blanket for your side of the bed.

  » Drinkers: If you regularly bring something to drink with you at bedtime, look for a nightstand with a glass or sealed stone top so that you don't leave water marks on the surface. Coasters can be messy, inconvenient to locate, and don't always work. Alternately, look for a nightstand with a built-in or pull-out tray that's easy to wipe and that disappears when not in use. Of course, you can always have a piece of glass cut for the top of your nightstand if it's wood or some other easy-to-mark material.

  » Readers: If you read before bedtime, look for a nightstand with enough room to neatly accommodate your reading material. For a cleaner appearance, or if you like to have a plethora of reading material at hand, look for a nightstand with shelves or drawers that can neatly store your goods below the surface. A drawer is also useful if you have reading glasses that mostly come out at bedtime.

  » Jewelry Wearers: If your nighttime ritual includes taking off delicate jewelry and watches before bedtime, look for a convenient drawer that can accommodate a jewelry box.

  » Medicine Takers and TV Watchers: Pillboxes and remotes are great to store in a top drawer for convenience's sake.

  » Workers: For those who like to have their technology bedside, a nightstand that doubles as a secondary desk is not a bad choice. For some folks, this might even be their primary desk if they don't have the space for another at-home work location.

- **Proportion counts:** Make sure that your nightstands are proportional to your bed size. A king-size bed should have proportionally bigger nightstands, or your nightstands will look oddly puny. A twin bed looks best paired with smaller nightstands that won't overwhelm the size of the bed.

- **Perfect pairings:** A pair of nightstands flanking a bed does not need to match. In fact, having a pair of non-matching nightstands is a great way to add a little personality to a bedroom and lets the individual on each side of the bed take their differing functional needs and aesthetic preferences into account. The key to making disparate nightstands work is to have some kind of visual link between the nightstands. This could be a color, material, style, metal finish, shape, or wood tone. Personally I'm fond of matching nightstands and the serenity, balance, and calming effect they create in the bedroom. That said mismatched stands could be aesthetically arresting, and quite interesting.

- **Make a connection:** Make sure that two "mismatched" nightstands are relatively similar in height and width so that your bedroom doesn't end up looking like a garage sale. Having a similar height is also good for ensuring that your bedside lamps will be about the same height, which is helpful functionally for reading purposes and helpful aesthetically if you have a pair of lamps. Even if you don't have a matched set of bedside lamps, I often find it visually discomforting to see two bedside lamps at dissimilar heights.

- **Skirt the issue:** For folks who are really short on storage, consider a leggy table covered with a tailored, top-to-floor table skirt. The skirt is a great way to get items out of sight that won't fit in drawers or behind cabinet doors, such as suitcases, a dog bed, or the decorative throw pillows that adorn the top of your bed when you're not sleeping in it.

MUSEUM
MUSEUM
ANIMAL STORIES
FAIRY TALES
FAIRY STORIES

BEDROOM STORAGE

Once you free yourself from the tyranny of the bedroom set, with its matchy-matchy, one-size-fits-all standard array of furniture, you can look for storage pieces that better suit your needs and speak to your design aesthetic. Mixing dresser styles and designs within a space creates a richer and more layered look that will ultimately have more visual endurance. Maintain a visual link, such as a general color palette or tonal similarities, between all of your dresser pieces so that they make sense together. Similar hardware can be another way to tie disparate pieces together.

Consider having multiple units of the same dresser sit side-by-side on a larger wall if this is the best space plan option for your room. It's an efficient way to get a lot of dresser storage in one place. In these instances, you will want your dressers to be as identical as possible, and you will want their sides to be flush. Dresser legs or tops that extend beyond the sides of the dresser will inhibit allowing two or more units to sit side-by-side with the visual appearance of one, so select your dresser style with that in mind. The choices for bedroom storage pieces are many:

- **Tallboy:** Tallboys typically consist of a wardrobe (something with doors) on the top supported by a chest of drawers on the bottom. Because they're a hybrid of both highboys and armoires, their sizing can range.

- **American Chiffonier:** This piece of furniture usually consists of a chest of drawers with a mirror attached to the top. For the most part, it's similarly sized to a chest of drawers.

- **Dressers or Extra Wide Dressers:** These pieces make excellent nightstands in smaller rooms that need efficiency in space planning, or in grand rooms that require appropriately large-scaled pieces. In these instances, make sure that the dresser is no deeper than 24 inches to prevent bumping into it as you make your way in and out of the bed. Additionally, it's best to have the dresser height relatively similar to the mattress height.

- **Armoires:** For those who still want a television hidden inside a piece of furniture, armoires and tallboys are good options that also provide additional storage for media components, clothing, and other items. Be sure that you know the inside dimensions of where you'd like to put your television. Furniture retailers and manufacturers usually provide the exterior dimensions online but not interior clearances, so if you think it's going to be close, it's best to go measure or ask before purchasing. Returning large pieces of furniture can be costly!

- **Lingerie Chests:** These tall, narrow dressers typically or traditionally have seven drawers, one for each day of the week. Modern versions can have just six drawers. You can use a lingerie chest in the traditional fashion, but they can store for any kind of clothing. If you're short on square footage, these slender chests can be quite useful. They are typically about 60 inches tall and 20 inches wide. Keep in mind they are taller than many dressers so they do take up visual space and they may be more noticeable than other storage solutions.

Although it may seem logical to fill a small room with vertical dresser pieces, such as highboys, tallboys, armoires, and lingerie chests, to take advantage of volume versus square footage, too many tall pieces in a small room can make the room feel boxed in and even smaller. Limit vertical pieces to two in a smaller bedroom, and consider using dressers in lieu of leggy nightstands and media units to provide for additional drawers.

LIGHTING:
IMPORTANT FACTS & FEATURES

Lighting is a critical element in a design scheme for what it delivers in terms of both function and aesthetics. Unfortunately, it is often one of the most overlooked and least considered, even in high-end homes and expensive design projects. It's ironic, because lighting is the element in a room most responsible for setting its ambiance and mood. When someone walks into a room and it feels good to them, 99% of the time it's because the lighting has been done properly. Moreover, there are so many amazing lighting options in the form of table and floor lamps, hanging fixtures, sconces, and recessed lighting that can support and tie into all the other design choices in your rooms. So when shopping for lighting, keep style, color, form, *and* function in mind.

RECESSED LIGHTING

I truly believe that recessed lighting is important to good design, so much so that, if you have the budget to retrofit recessed cans into your ceiling, it's worth doing. There may be people who disagree with me about the necessity of recessed lighting, and I respect that. However, in my opinion, recessed lighting *is* essential in every room as it can help set a room's mood and atmosphere. I also like rooms to be evenly lit, and controllable via dimmer switches—two more benefits of recessed lighting. You can retrofit recessed lighting almost anywhere. For instance, we were able to retrofit recessed lighting into my circa 1925 home in Atlanta.

It is much more difficult to create the ambiance you want in a room without every form of lighting to help, and that starts with recessed lighting. There are those who feel recessed lighting is inelegant (I disagree), but they are efficient and functional, providing a consistent, overall light level in a room. Trim kits, the outer border that finishes the light, are available in white, black, and standard metal finishes, so they can blend with the ceiling color, helping the cans to disappear. When installed with dimmers, as all lights should be, they can be adjusted to whatever is happening outside. On a dark and gloomy day they can be bright, or in the evening, they can be turned down to make the space a little more romantic and cozy. As I said earlier, most builders use 6-inch cans for their economy and accessibility, but I prefer a 4-inch or smaller can because as they can be less obtrusive and just as functional.

TRIM KITS FOR RECESSED LIGHTING

- **General Recessed Lighting:** I like a general trim kit with a white trim ring and a clear silver interior cone for white or light-colored ceilings. This unobtrusive combination directs the most light where you want it. For very dark or black ceilings, choose a black trim ring paired with either a clear silver or black interior cone. Be aware that a black cone will be less noticeable, but will not direct as much light into the room.
- **Wall Washing or General Art Lighting:** For this purpose, I think a white Slot Diffuser is a clean and nice way to go. Point the slot in the direction of the artwork (lining it up directly is best) to help illuminate the wall or the art hanging on that wall.
- **Directed Art Lighting:** When I highlight a piece of art, I much prefer a Gimbal Ring Trim, which allows for rotation of your actual bulb toward the art. The Gimbal Ring sits below the surface of the ceiling and is more of a visual distraction than a simple Slot Diffuser, but it allows a more precise light placement. As with the General Trim and the Slot Diffuser Trim, choose a white or light metal Gimbal Ring Trim for white or light-colored ceilings and a black or dark metal ring for dark-colored ceilings.

FLUSH MOUNTED FIXTURES

These fixtures have an understated presence in a room, hugging the ceiling with some kind of dome, globe, or box often made from glass, but other materials are also used. Basically, a flush mount goes straight from the canopy to the fixture, with no stem to drop the fixture down from the ceiling. In older homes with low ceilings, a ceiling mount fixture may be the only option for ease of movement through the space or if the space above the ceiling surface can't accommodate the hardware required to install recessed lighting. When choosing a ceiling mount fixture with visible trim, think about predominate tones and other metals in the room and choose something compatible.

PENDANTS & HANGING FIXTURES

Hanging fixtures can make a dramatic statement in a room simply because of their suspended nature, which often places them at or above eye level. Pendants and hanging fixtures vary widely in style, from traditional multi-armed brass chandeliers dripping with crystal prisms to mouth-blown, singleshade Italian globes in dramatic colors. Every decade and style type has associated iconic hanging fixture forms, and this offers great opportunities for finding the right light to reinforce your overall room style. Let's review the critical distances for pendant and hanging fixtures we learned in Chapter One. Remember to always measure from the pendant's lowest point:

- **66":** Measurement when placing a pendant above the dining room table, desk, library table, game table, or any other 29 to 30 inch high table you will be seated at, from the finished floor to the lowest point of the fixture. This allows for proper illumination of the table surface while still allowing people to see each other across the table. Also note that, for tables up to 6 feet in length, one fixture is sufficient. Tables that exceed 72 inches may need multiple fixtures with separate junction boxes or a single fixture that spans the correct length of the table to adequately illuminate the surface of the table.

  The size and shape of your table determines the lighting fixture or fixtures. Fixtures above a round table should never exceed the diameter of the table itself. For rectangular or ovals tables, single or multiple fixtures should not exceed three-quarters of the overall length of the table, including chairs, nor the overall width of the table. Alternatively, if the table does not have chairs at its head and foot, the fixtures may run its entire length.

- **6":** Measurement when placing a hanging fixture over a bed, the fixture should be 6 inches above head level when seated in your bed. Because bed frame and mattress heights vary significantly, there is no exact measurement that can be given without these components in place. Hanging fixtures with a minimum of 6 inch of head clearance, when you are in a seated position in your bed, keeps you from bumping it accidentally.

- **36"** to **40":** Measurement when placing pendants over a kitchen island, from top of island countertop to underside of fixture, to allow for illumination and unobstructed visibility.

- **66"** to **76":** Measurement from finished floor when placing a pendant above a coffee table. If you need to walk under it or see a high-mounted television, make sure to clear these functional needs.

- **76"** to **78":** The minimum measurement in a hallway or other open space, from finished floor to the lowest point of the fixture, to allow for comfortable passage for most homes with ceilings that are 114 inches (9 feet, 6 inches) or lower.

- **84":** For ceiling heights at or greater than 114 inches (or 9 feet, 6 inches), hang fixtures at 84 inches from finished floor to the lowest point to ensure complete ease for all but a few people. It's not so high that the light is not functional, and the light stays in proportion to the height of the room. Hanging fixtures higher than this height do not allow the fixture to be appreciated and keeps the light too high. Of course, there are always exceptions, i.e., when you have a double story entryway or room, or ceilings that are higher than 14 feet. You may have to adjust accordingly.

TABLE & FLOOR LAMPS

Table and floor lamps are the most versatile of lighting features in a room because of the sheer variety of sizes and shapes, and because they can easily be moved. They can also be less costly than hard-wired or permanently installed lighting—but not always. Designer lamps can command very high prices, especially those that are fashionable and in demand, or made from costly materials. On the other hand, affordable and beautiful lamps can be found in many home stores, antique shops (always have an old lamp's wiring checked), and department stores. Lamps also inject color and form into a room, especially those that have inherent sculptural qualities. As for function, strategically placed lamps help set a mood and can act as task lighting, especially when situated within a reading nook or area, on a sofa table, or on side tables.

LEARN FROM VERN

BULB SMART

- Incandescent bulbs have traditionally been the least expensive and most commonly used bulbs for household use. I recommend 60-75 watts for general, overall lighting in most living spaces. This is also a great choice for most recessed cans. I lean towards 60 watts for most lamps used for reading. Use 75-100 watts in garages, pantries, closets, and anyplace you need bright task lighting. A low 40 watt bulb is good for creating ambience and setting a mood.

- LED bulbs are more environmentally friendly than incandescent, and they've come a long way from when they were first on the market. LEDs now offer the warm incandescent feeling we all appreciate. Making the switch can be a little confusing. Start by choosing a dimmable LED and look for three qualities: Lumens (light output), Color, and Color Rendering Index (CRI), which quantitatively measures an artificial light's accuracy in showing colors compared to a natural light source. For an LED bulb comparable to incandescent, look for a color of 2700 degrees Kelvin (warm) and a CRI above 90. Eight-hundred lumen LEDs (comparable to 60 watts) are broadly usable but 1100 lumens better approximate 75 watt incandescent bulbs; 450 lumen LEDs better approximate 40 watts.

- Halogen bulbs most closely approximate the spectrum of the sun and produce a crisp, white light that's great for lighting art. When installing recessed halogen lighting, guard against using diameters greater than 4 inches to ensure minimal visual distraction.

- Compact fluorescent bulbs don't produce a quality of light that suits interior design in my opinion, and for that reason I'm not a fan of these bulbs. They are acceptable in garages and for purely utilitarian spaces—but I don't really like to even use them there.

- Whichever bulb you choose, be cautious about not exceeding the wattage level intended for a fixture; that information should be written somewhere on the fixture itself. Exceeding the wattage level is dangerous and could be a fire hazard. Going below the wattage recommendation is generally not a problem.

ART:
IMPORTANT FACTS & FEATURES

Artwork plays such an important part of my design aesthetic. Specifically, Craig and I collect fine art photography as well as objects from our travels that offer both beauty and a reminder of the places we've been. Art gives rooms personality, color, and texture. Not only should artwork itself have an intrinsic beauty (not necessarily "value" in terms of expense), but it should always express something about you, too. I love finding art pieces on my travels and have shipped back all sorts of things, from large paintings to interesting sculptures, from the places I've been. When someone remarks upon a piece of art in my home, I can tell him a story about it. That's something you can't do if you just went to a mall and bought a picture that matches your sofa. I understand it's not possible to find every piece of meaningful artwork you'd like to have in a space, and that there is a need for "placeholders" until the perfect thing materializes. That's part of the design journey. Here are some ideas to keep in mind when buying art:

- **Make an Emotional Connection:** An art piece should "speak" to you. Buy what you like, and take your time choosing. You don't have to fill up a wall just for the sake of filling a wall.
- **Harmonize:** Color and texture in art you select should support the color and texture scheme in the room where it will be placed, which is not the same as matching a piece of art to a sofa.
- **Choose the Right Backdrop:** If you love art and have a lot of it, or plan on collecting art, choose neutral wall colors that allow the art to take center stage.
- **Go Local:** Original art can be affordable *as well as* a great investment if you seek out local artists at group shows, galleries, and community art fairs.
- **Format Bargains:** Consider photography, drawings, and limited edition prints as another affordable way of acquiring original art.
- **Map It:** Large old maps can be amazing stand-ins for "real" art, especially if you track one down of your town, city, or state, or places that are meaningful to you for any reason.
- **Scale:** Go big. Although there are many beautifully made small-scale art pieces, and it is often easier to transport smaller items, large-scale art can have more of an impact on the design, character, and feel of a room.
- **Look for the Practical:** Look at art opportunities that go beyond paintings, photographs, and sculpture. Art can be something that serves a function other than aesthetic. Great lamps, a beautiful pendant fixture, a wonderfully detailed box to store remotes or keys, or a handsome rug are all ways you can bring artistic flair to a room while fulfilling a needed function.
- **Present it Well:** Give art the ability to communicate how beautiful and wonderful it is to you. Don't crowd a room with too many things, because it's harder to appreciate individual pieces. Give precious art objects an opportunity to breathe by ensuring that they don't have too much competition. Think of how a museum displays important objects! Art that is lit correctly, displayed on a pedestal or base, or showcased in a clear box commands attention and is easier to take in.

LEARN FROM VERN

TRAVEL SIZE

I believe in bringing decorative items and furnishings back from trips abroad. My general philosophy is to buy one or two big things that act as permanent reminders of the specific journey I'm on. That requires forethought. If I want a rug for a certain room and I am going to Turkey, I figure out how big the rug needs to be before I get on the plane. If I find one I like and it's not the right size, it doesn't make sense to buy it. Or, I may be interested in a large wood carving from a trip to Asia. I have to consider the general dimensions of the wall and the room where it will be installed, as well as the color palette of the room. I keep that information on my Smartphone or in a pocket notebook so it's never out of reach. This strategy is very deliberate, and quite different from the natural tendency to pack your suitcase with small souvenirs that end up cluttering a side table or bookshelf that lacks cohesion.

Avoid this trap by looking for larger statement pieces—you're much better off paying to ship one big thing that will actually remind you of your journey and serve an important design purpose. Airlines can be surprisingly accommodating: I hauled a 10 x 14-foot rug back from India—the good people at Delta Airlines folded it up for me and put it right on the plane. I've packed 45 yards of silk from Thailand into my suitcase. I never let scale intimidate me when I'm on the road. When I go on a major trip abroad, I bring a large and empty suitcase that accommodates another, slightly smaller and empty suitcase. When there is potential for bringing great stuff back, the cost of checking one or even two extra bags is miniscule compared to shipping costs.

WINDOW TREATMENTS:
IMPORTANT FACTS & FEATURES

Window treatments come in a variety of styles and materials—from simple linen shades to wooden shutters to floor-length draperies. Deciding what you want in a room depends on the style of the overall space, the size and shape of the windows, and whether you want the window treatments to function as light-controlling features or as a decorative feature, or as both.

- **Roman shades:** These can be soft and traditional or structured and contemporary. They can be made from virtually any fabric, including lined silk, cotton, linen, or a blend. These shades can soften the look of a space via the choice of fabric. They are also good for windows that sit right against the end of a wall, where the corner prevents you from using side panels. However, Roman shades don't offer as much control over the light that comes into a room when compared to an adjustable slatted blind. When lined with a black out fabric, they make a room very dark when drawn down, which may be an asset in a bedroom.

- **Panels:** These treatments can be pleated or held up with grommets or a simple rod pocket—are popular because they offer a chance to add softness, texture, pattern, and color to a room. Panels are my favorite kind of window treatments, especially when hung from the top of the wall, at or near the ceiling. They are critical to the completeness of a room's look. I generally pair them with blinds for light control, allowing the drapery panels to play the starring decorative role on the window. Full-length panels unify a space, especially one that has different-sized windows. They help bring that thread of continuity in your design. When choosing readymade panels or fabric, or if you are having them made, decide whether you want voluminous panels or sleek, straight panels. For full panels, lighter weight fabrics such as cotton, lightweight silks, and lightweight linens are good choices. For a contemporary feel, look for wool, heavier weight silks and linen, and even mohair can be dramatic as well as luxurious. Polyester blends are also a great choice, since they help color fastness and wrinkle resistance. If you have southern exposure and love sunny rooms, a silk or linen is going to decompose and fade from sunlight. A poly blend helps prevent this from happening. Textile advancements mean you often can't tell the difference between pure materials and a blend.

- **Balloon shades:** These are similar to roman shades in their operation, but are characterized by a voluminous fullness appropriate for very traditional settings.
- **Sheers:** Translucent panels can be used with opaque panels or on their own. Sheers diffuse light while still allowing it to filter through, but since they offer no privacy, be careful how and where you use them.
- **Plantation shutters:** These are usually made from wood or a wood composite and offer a very neat, clean look in a room. They can also be used with panels; however, panels are not necessary with plantation shutters. Interior shutters have limited light control, but when closed, do shut out light. I find these shutters to be bulky and limiting, so I avoid them.
- **Blinds and shades:** Simple and modern, these single panel shades can be pulled down to shut out all light and lifted up to let the sunshine in. Slatted blinds give many more options for light control than shades and shutters, depending on how you adjust the slats. They can be used on their own or with panels, sheers, or a cornice. However, blinds used on their own often give a room an incomplete look, so I prefer to use them in partnership with panels or another soft or fabric treatment. When selecting blinds, choose wood slats that coordinate with your trim. That is, if you have white window trim, choose white wood slatted blinds.
- **Cornice:** This is a constructed frame that is usually upholstered. Cornices offer a formal look, although they can look quite contemporary, depending on the fabric and trim used. A cornice can neatly cover the hardware associated with hanging drapes, which is helpful if your hardware is purely functional and not that attractive.

RUGS:
IMPORTANT FACTS & FEATURES

Rugs add warmth, color, and texture to a room. They are also useful in delineating conversation areas in large, open plan spaces. Rugs also come in a dizzying array of styles and materials, from traditional Turkish wool to contemporary flat, woven jute.

- **Cover story:** If you want a rug to cover the floor of a room, measure the room's width and length and then subtract 2 to 3 feet from each side. That is the size rug you should look for—or as close to that size as possible. If you can't find the right room-sized rug ready-made, consider having carpeting cut to size and bound.

- **Wool is wonderful:** It's a great fabric for rugs: soft, durable, and cozy. But all wool is not created equal. Just because a rug is made from wool doesn't guarantee it is a good-quality rug. Look for density of pile, and how many knots per square inch the rug has—in general, the more knots the higher the quality. Look for a minimum of 120 to 330 of knots per inch or "KPSI." Eighty KPSI or fewer is generally poor quality, and anything higher than 330 KPSI is considered to be very fine.

- **Go natural:** Materials like jute, sisal, and sea grass are affordable and can go with almost any color scheme. Remember, however, that these rugs lend a casual air to a room, and often feel scratchy underfoot. They offer a great look for a beach house; however, I confess I don't have any of these kinds of rugs at my beach house. It is difficult to remove dirt from the material, and vacuums have a hard time getting debris out of the weave, which is something to take into consideration if you, like me, don't like a rug to be a crumb collector.

- **Flat is fun:** Flat woven wool or cotton kilim or dhurrie rugs come in a variety of patterns and colors, from traditional to modern. They add a fun color feature to a room, but again, they are casual and laid back, so not usually used in more formal settings. However, very fine examples of antique kilims can certainly find a home in formal spaces. Be aware that these rugs are thinner than wool or nylon pile rugs, and may not hold up as well over time.

- **Nylon is nice:** There are pros and cons to both nylon and wool, but when it comes to long-term durability and stain resistance, I'm a fan of high quality nylon. Many nylons are now so advanced they mimic the softness and patina of wool. Many nylon fibers on the market are resistant to bacteria, they won't fade as fast as natural fiber rugs, and they are easier to clean, as many are stain resistant. It's worth considering this material, even if you have a bias against it.

- **Center trouble:** A rug with a center medallion is almost never a good idea because it automatically dictates where everything must be placed—around the medallion!

- **Textures and patterns:** A solid or textured rug, or one with an overall pattern gives you more freedom, and this is an important factor when designing a room. When thinking about all-over patterns, think about the scale as it relates to the fabrics in your room. If you have a tight, small pattern on drapes and soft furnishings, a larger-scale pattern on the rug may work better, and vice versa.

- **Pad it:** Don't forget to buy a rug pad that's right for your rug material and size. A pad protects and lengthens the life of both your rug and your floor. It also helps keep the rug in place, and prevents it from shifting and moving.

OUTDOOR LIVING SPACE:

IMPORTANT FACTS & FEATURES

If you haven't looked for outdoor furniture lately, you're in for a pleasant surprise. While you can still find folding, webbed lawn chairs and picnic tables, the variety of great-looking, comfortable, and functional outdoor lounge chairs, sofas, chaises, daybeds, and dining tables and chairs is almost as wide as it is for indoor furniture. From traditional to contemporary, outdoor furniture makes it very easy to coordinate your indoor and outdoor rooms. Maintain your interior décor style as you shop for and pull together your exterior décor so that there is a cohesive and seamless transition from one to the other.

- **Outdoor Furniture:** Almost every type of furniture that is made for the inside is also now available for the outside. The full array of outdoor living and dining furniture, from side tables and sofa tables to buffets and cocktail tables, are available in a wide variety of styles. Interesting innovations in materials now translate to fully upholstered sofas and chairs with the linen look, resin wicker that withstands inclement weather beautifully, and the look of leather for your outdoor den that matches the real leather in your indoor den. Even outdoor beds are now widely available, making it possible to now fully stretch out during outdoor siestas. If you live in a mild climate, you can use vintage or new, painted indoor furniture in sheltered areas.

- **Put Down a Rug:** Rugs made out of fade-resistant acrylic and other durable materials suited for exterior use are a great foundation for your outdoor living and dining spaces. Rugs help give outdoor rooms a finished look, and as on the inside, they delineate seating and other activity areas beautifully. Make sure your outdoor rugs are substantial enough to accommodate the furniture that's on them. Just because it's outdoors doesn't mean that you can get away with using a rug that's too small.

- **Consider Drapery:** If you have a place to hang them, such as a pergola or porch columns, outdoor draperies lend elegance and needed shade to exterior living spaces. Choose materials that are mold, mildew, and fade resistant. That means looking at fabrics specifically designated for outdoor use. Drapery hardware designated for outside use is crucial as well. Stainless steel and anodized aluminum are good options.

- **Soften Seating with Throw Pillows and Throws:** Exterior options for outdoor pillows and throws have multiplied exponentially. This is where you can and should inject bold colors and patterns. When it comes to selecting upholstery, I much prefer a neutral because of its versatility and timelessness. It can be costly to replace or reupholster. The bold color can come through pillows, throws, and other soft accessories. Colorful accessories fool the eye into thinking that the entire space is colorful. Moreover, these smaller pieces can easily and affordably change with the seasons or with your taste, while the neutral background of your furniture remains steadfast and dependable. With the proliferation of so many more fabrics that are resistant to mold, mildew, and fading, creating visual interest with interesting patterns and textures through these elements makes decorating outside as much fun as it is inside.

- **Accessorize:** Using decorative accessories outside are a great way to fully convert those spaces into extensions of your indoor home. Accessories don't have to be labeled for exterior use for you to use them outside. Objects in heavier duty ceramic, concrete, stainless steel, and anodized aluminum can all be used outdoors for at least a part of the year. Some objects aren't resistant to freezing temperatures, so be sure to bring those in before temperatures drop too low. Additionally, objects that are lightweight might not sustain heavier winds, so ensure that you don't decorate with those objects outside or that you bring them in when inclement weather is coming.

- **Garden Stools:** These are among the most versatile pieces of furniture in the marketplace. They are a great way to inject punches of color into a neutral seating arrangement, and a bit of whimsy too. Select ceramic or rust-resistant metal garden stools that are between 17 to 20 inches in height to be used as exterior side tables and overflow seating. Garden stools can be cleaned up and brought inside when the weather turns unpleasant. They look equally smart, indoors or out.

- **Exterior Hurricanes:** Nothing quite matches the ambiance created by the flicker of candlelight at an outdoor dinner or party. Exterior hurricanes in a wide variety of sizes, made out of stainless steel, teak, or some other outdoor-friendly material, are a wonderful way to add interesting and sculptural forms to your outside living areas that also protect the flicker of the candles.

- **Lighting:** Extend the use of your exterior living spaces with lighting specifically rated for outdoor use. A wide array of chandeliers, pendants, sconces, and table and floor lamps are now available to use in protected and unprotected areas to help complete the look of your outdoor areas.

- **Heaters:** Make outdoor entertaining even more long-lasting by using an outdoor heater. Most free-standing propane heaters on the market have a heating range that is approximately 3 to 5 feet or less when used in cold, windy weather. Small tabletop models may only provide warmth within a couple of feet of the heater. If you want to heat a large area, experts advise placing multiple heaters 8 to 20 feet apart.

CHAPTER THREE:

PULLING IT ALL TOGETHER—MAKING A ROOM YOUR OWN

HOW TO CREATE THE PERFECT SETTING

Now comes the fun: making a space into a room you and your family can enjoy and live in for years. In this chapter we talk about color and explore ways to create and execute floor plans that are warm and inviting, while also providing ample space for navigating. We also take a detailed look at how to use accessories, art, and flowers to bring personality and life to a room. So important!

PAINT:
FUNCTION, PERSONALITY & BEAUTY

Painting a room is often said to be one of the easiest, affordable ways to update your home and express your individuality. But it can get expensive if you choose the wrong color and have to buy more paint and take time (or hire someone) to paint again. Everyone has had that experience, including me: "Oh, it's not really what I wanted. Back to the paint department." Selecting the right paint color can be daunting, as the choice of color and finish seems inexhaustible. If you keep a few guidelines in mind, you can end paint paralysis, and come up with a perfect palette without "painter's remorse."

PAINT BASICS

Paint is an ancient substance; over the millennia, it's been made from ground-up bugs, dust, and vegetative matter. Some paints are milk-based. But today's home decorator typically chooses between oil-based and latex paints. Oil-based paint is more durable than latex, and for that reason is often used for exterior painting; however, it is much more difficult and time-consuming to work with than latex. My best advice is to leave oil-based paint to the paint professionals.

Latex paint is the far better choice for interior walls you paint yourself because of its easy application and soap and water clean up. In general, I try to stick to low or no VOC (Volatile Organic Compounds) latex paint since it tends to be more environmentally friendly. Low or no-VOC paint is virtually odorless, too.

Before you even think about color, make a decision about which paint finish is best for your project. Paint finishes range from light-absorbing flat and matte to eggshell, which has a very faint sheen, to semi-gloss, gloss, and enamel, all of which successively increase the shine factor.

Flat, matte, or eggshell finishes can be pretty much used interchangeably. The main difference is that flat and matte finishes can be more difficult to clean, so in high-traffic areas or in kids' spaces, you might want to opt for eggshell, which can be wiped clean with a damp cloth. Flat and matte finishes are more forgiving of a wall's imperfections, so use them on older plaster walls or any wall that doesn't have pristine or smooth sheetrock. Flat and matte surfaces are good for living rooms and adult bedrooms: in other words, the places where grown-ups hang out. Some manufacturers make wipable flat and matte finishes, which means you can use these paints in many other rooms. Eggshell, because of its quick-clean surface, is great for places that everybody uses: kitchens, bathrooms, kids' bedrooms, and family rooms.

QUICK GUIDE TO WHERE EACH FINISH WORKS BEST:

- **Bathroom and Kitchen Walls and Bath Ceilings:** For areas in direct proximity to water or humidity, an eggshell finish can be wiped and is resistant to moisture. If you like the look of a matte finish, you can find these water-friendly properties built into a flat paint.

- **Ceilings:** Most of the time, a flat or matte finish is best. Like your walls, ceiling surfaces have a good amount of irregularities that get enhanced with higher sheens. For the most part, ceilings don't get a lot of wear and tear, so performance on this surface is not as critical. There are exceptions, though. For spaces with low ceilings, a higher sheen surface gives the perception of higher ceilings. Gloss paint on a ceiling can be both dramatic and beautiful, but be sure to first smooth out as many imperfections on your ceiling surface as possible because they will be noticeable under a shiny surface.

- **Kids' Room Walls:** Consider an eggshell finish in the rooms that little people spend the most time in for easier cleaning of handprints, fingerprints, scuffs, and other kid-generated marks.

  Walls are the most typical surfaces to paint, but ceilings, trim, paintable floor surfaces, and furniture all offer opportunities to add unexpected color that lends another layer to a cohesive design scheme, and expresses your individuality and personality.

- **Trim:** Painting your trim a higher sheen than the adjacent wall, such as semi-gloss or gloss, is a great way to highlight the architectural detailing of molding. Baseboards and windowsills also experience more contact with hands, shoes, and vacuum cleaners so the highly durable and easy-to-wipe finish of a gloss surface has a practical benefit.

- **Floors:** When painting wood, concrete, or other paintable floor surfaces, make sure you use a product specifically designed for the floor, such as porch paint, along with the proper prep-work, including sanding and priming. This ensures that your painted floor endures the wear and tear of foot traffic. Paint designed for other surfaces in your home don't necessarily exhibit these same properties.

- **Furniture:** Furniture comes into contact with human hands more so than most walls, so employ an eggshell, semi-gloss, or gloss finish when painting it. Prep surfaces by cleaning and sanding well so paint adheres properly. If you like a softer look on furniture, look for milk and chalk paints, which offer a soft matte finish that can be given a soft sheen with paste wax.

THE ANIMAL BOOK
JENKINS

COLOR BASICS

There is an almost limitless array of paint colors to select from nowadays; technology even lets you create your own custom color based on a swatch of fabric or a certain shade torn from the pages of a magazine. People love to pick a room's paint color first because they can easily imagine the significant change that happens quickly with a fresh coat of paint. Admittedly, that's exciting. But then they're forced to work around the color they chose, trying to fit all the other elements in the room around it. Choosing a paint color first means that you then have to find rugs, fabrics, and artwork to work with that color. What if you already have a great rug that doesn't work with what you've chosen? Here are some tips for choosing color:

- **Limiting Factors.** Look first at the most limiting factors you know will be used in a room, and choose a paint color based on those items. For instance, rugs and artwork are two elements that oftentimes can't be readily changed, especially if you have an emotional attachment to these items. They might be valuable, meaningful, or antiques . . . or they just might be the objects that have the most number of colors in them. You also often have the fewest choices with these two elements, so they narrow down the colors and shades you must choose between. I see that as a great benefit, since the wide choice of colors available can be overwhelming and confusing.

- **Meaningful Objects.** If you're starting with a blank slate, find an item that inspires you or represents what you want to accomplish in the room. This can be a fabulous rug or a great piece of art; even a vase or lamp can serve this purpose. Or, it might be a beautiful piece of fabric that may end up being used on accent pillows—but it still offers a pleasing color palette that helps you identify shades and tones for the room.

- **Inspiration.** To get a general idea of the color family you'd like to be in (blue, red, beige, etc.), thumb through magazines and design books to tag images you like. They don't have to be rooms or specifically paint colors. They can really be any images that make you feel the way you want to feel in that room. You can even select family photos or objects in your home that you love. After doing that, see if you can distinguish a common color thread that links these disparate images and objects together. Give yourself a mini-quiz:

  » Are your colors airy and light filled?

  » Or are they exotic, dark, and adventurous?

  » Do you gravitate toward images that have water in them?

  » Are you attracted to greens, browns, and mossy colors?

  » Are your colors "warm" (oranges, browns, reds, cream) or "cool" (blue, green, metallic, white)?

- **Sample it.** Once you hone in on the common color thread, you have a direction, and the color choice should become more obvious. At your paint or home improvement store, start selecting paint swatches that are in the range of what you are thinking about.

- **Consider alternatives.** Start by picking the colors you really like, and then select a few lighter and darker hues than you might normally be comfortable with. You should even dare yourself to pick a few that are completely different from what you were initially thinking but that you're kind of gravitating towards. Paper swatches of each color are generally free, so bring home a broad spectrum of hues that you think might work.
- **Lighting Conditions.** Keep in mind that the lighting at the store is different from what you have at home, so what looks good under institutional lighting might not look so good at home.
- **Edit.** After you've assembled your paper paint swatches at home, tape them on the walls of the room you are painting and look at them during various parts of the day. The color will change depending on the mix of artificial and natural light in the space. What you liked at the paint store might look completely different in your room. Live with these paper swatches for a couple of days and start taking down the ones you definitely don't care for until you're left with the one you're most happy with. If you can't get it down to one, at least get it down to the two or three that you think could work.
- **Try out colors.** When you think you have the color you want, or have two to three strong contenders, purchase inexpensive sample pots of your choices. These usually cost just a few dollars and allow you to paint a 3-foot square of your surface, the minimum size required to get the best indication of how the color will look in the room.
- **Judge when dry.** Wait until the samples are completely dry before making a decision. Dry paint looks dramatically different than it did when you first applied it to the wall. Sometimes people panic when they first roll on a color because it looks so much brighter or more intense than it appeared on the original paper sample. Don't panic and don't make a decision based on this. Wait until it dries, and you will see the true shade. Paint on your walls will always look a little darker over a large area than it does on a small paper swatch.
- **Think twice, finalize once.** Don't be surprised if you have to go back and adjust a little based on the 3-foot trial squares on your walls. If sample pots aren't available, you can always purchase quarts of the colors to try out. This is a little more expensive, but much cheaper and less time consuming in the long run than painting your room a color that you don't like.

COLOR AS A THREAD OF CONTINUITY

The eclectic and curated look in home design is here to stay. Gone are the days when the expectation was for us to purchase everything in sets. The uninteresting uniformity of living room sets, dining rooms sets, and bedroom sets have made way to mixing furniture and accessories that reflect the specialness of individuality as discussed above. But how do you visually tie together everything in a room and between and among rooms so that your home doesn't end up looking decorated from a junky garage sale?

I had to learn this the hard way. I hadn't been out of grad school for very long when I moved into an apartment where I could finally paint the walls any way I wanted. It was a chance to try hues and tones that interested me, and I wasted no time painting every room, from hallway to kitchen to living room and bedroom, a different and unrelated color. The result? It was like living in a circus tent. Any of the colors I chose would have been fine individually, but having them all in one apartment was not very pleasant. Since I was living on the meager salary of an intern, I was too broke to afford several more gallons of paint to correct my mistake. I had to live with this riot of color for quite a while.

As it happens, this period also marked the beginning of my collecting; I was making sacrifices so I could afford a few good pieces of art and furniture. Unfortunately, the colors in my small place so were unrelated, they fought with the pieces I had brought into the space. Lesson learned. You have to keep in mind how one color is going to relate to another color in an adjacent room or area. Consider your end goal, such as how your collections will work throughout these spaces. Wall colors in a space should feel intentional, like a complete thought.

Having a thread of continuity becomes important to tying disparate items together so that the overall room makes sense. Color is one of my preferred threads of continuity. Reiterating one or two colors within a space gives you more latitude to then vary the styles and content within a room. If you move towards incorporating a multitude of colors, it's necessary to have other threads of continuity (such as style) to prevent the room from feeling haphazard.

- **Flow.** Consider the flow of your home when employing multiple paint colors. Even if you don't have an open space plan, your home should easily flow from one space to the next.

- **Room to Room.** When painting a room, look at the adjoining room, and that can be a guide how to paint the room you are in if you're planning on painting the next room.

- **An overall color plan.** Give some thought to how colors look adjacent to each other and how many different colors you want to employ on a single level.

- **End on the inside corner.** When you do change wall color within a space, make sure that the color change happens on the inside corner of where two walls meet. Changing colors on an outside corner is difficult to execute perfectly and creates the impression that your wall is two-dimensional and insubstantial.

- **Go monochromatic.** In a small room, go monochromatic. From the walls to the drapes to furnishings, stay with the same tone. The smaller the room, the less contrast you want. The quickest way to make a small room smaller is to add a lot of contrast.

- **Differentiate with accents.** If you live in an open-space home and there is no logical place to change color from room to room, paint all walls the same color, and create differentiation through drape colors, furniture colors, or rug colors from room to room.

TODAY
BOUCHON • BAKERY

PUT COLOR IN ITS PLACE

Color has or should have a hierarchy in a well-designed room. Here, some guidlines to keep in mind.

- **Beware the accent wall.** Too many contrasting colors in a room are hard to live with. The number one mistake I see in both hotel rooms and in homes is the "accent wall"—a wall painted in a high contrast color to the other three walls. They make small hotels rooms appear even smaller. However, accent walls are often used in today's homes with open floor plans to define functional areas of space. They become the de facto focal point of a room, which can be tricky when there is a competing natural focal point such as a fireplace or picture window. My best advice about accent walls is to proceed with caution: avoid the two-focal point trap because your room will feel disjointed and confusing. Accent walls also tend to chop up rooms, making them feel smaller and less complete than if the entire room were painted uniformly. This is ironic, given that an open floor plan creates the entirely opposite effect! If you are going to have an accent wall, the color should terminate at an inside corner, not an outside corner.

- **Go dark?** Small rooms are often painted white or light colors in an effort to make them feel larger. This doesn't have to be the case. The important thing to remember with a small space is to keep it fairly monochromatic so that the eye effortlessly travels from surface to surface. This means purposefully limiting the colors of your largest items like paint, drapery fabric, and major furniture pieces to a tight range so that they blend into each other instead of dramatically sticking out. Dark colors are also often helpful in small spaces because they tend to eat the shadows created by light. Shadows are dark...even on white walls...so dark walls can help eliminate the definition of space created by shadows.

- **Streamline your color.** When every color in a room has equal weight, there is no cohesion or flow. Use no more than two or three bold colors in a room, and use them as supporting players to a lighter or more muted background. Bold choices need neutral blacks, whites, taupe, and browns to let them shine. Then, these color accents feel like precious jewels that dot the field.

- **Highlight quality art.** Generally, if you have great art or beautiful things, the walls don't need to do a lot of work. Bright wall colors will distract the eye from what you really want to be noticed: the art and/or the furnishings. Deep, saturated wall color or pale colors (think "gallery white") are the best choice when you want your art or other elements to take center stage.

- **Wall color can be art.** If you don't have great art, the wall color can do some of the heavy lifting in a room. In this case, brighter hues can be an antidote to your less-than-museum-quality framed prints and basic furnishings.

- **Paint some stripes!** This is a simple effect anyone can accomplish with a few basic tools (tape measure, painters tape, pencil). Horizontal stripes are great for widening a room, and are an effective way to visually link two spaces. Vertical stripes are good for rooms with low ceilings, as they increase the perception of height or volume. Tone on tone stripes add elegant architectural integrity to a room. For a classic look, choose a color and then go either up or down one on the paint strip for the second color. Or, use the same color in two different finishes (i.e., flat and semi-gloss). Very high constrast stripes are not effective in small spaces, but they can be graphic and fun when space is not a concern. I have a kitchen with classic black and white stripes that helps unify its two connected spaces.

CEILINGS, LOW AND HIGH

- **Rx for Low Ceilings.** The same color painted onto a horizontal surface (like a ceiling) will always look slightly darker than when it's painted onto a vertical surface (like a wall), so by painting the ceiling a slightly lighter version of the wall color, it effectively looks like it is the same color as the wall, thus dissipating the break where wall and ceiling meet. This creates the illusion of a higher ceiling. This trick doesn't work as well if you have crown molding, unless you paint your crown the same color as your wall.

- **Thinking through White.** Painting your ceilings bright white doesn't necessarily make them feel higher, unless your walls are also white. Otherwise, the contrast between wall and white ceiling calls attention to the ceiling, which may not be your intended result.

- **Rx for Angled Ceilings.** Cathedral ceilings and odd angled walls created by the underside of rooflines on top-level rooms are often painted the ceiling color, which is usually white. This creates such an odd visual condition because you then have an emphasis on an oddly short wall or a strange break in color. In almost all cases, it's better to paint these ceilings the same color as your wall. The room will feel more unified and complete in its design thought.

- **Rx for Tray Ceilings.** The vertical surfaces of tray ceilings present unique challenges. The tray ceiling is its own entity and should be treated in its entirety as the ceiling. Pick one of two routes: paint the short vertical surfaces that are part of the tray ceiling the same color as the rest of the tray and ceiling color, or paint both the vertical and horizontal the color of the wall to increase the sense of volume in a room.

PAPER VS. PAINT

Wallpaper is a viable and fashionable alternative today—gone are the cows and roosters, dainty floral repeats, and pastel stripes. Well, they aren't actually gone, but the selection of wallpaper styles has broadened considerably to include hand-printed motifs, modern graphics, wallpaper made from actual wood veneer, and wallpaper with beading, stitching, and other three-dimensional effects. If you don't have a lot of meaningful art in a room and are not planning on spending your resources that way, beautiful wallpaper can be a stand-in for wall art.

Personally, I think if you choose beautiful wallpaper, it should stand on its own and become the feature and focus of the wall where it's installed. Be cautious of hanging anything too busy on it as it will compete with the wallpaper pattern. I have amazing wood veneer wallpaper on a stairway at my Rosemary Beach house, and I've chosen to keep that wall otherwise unadorned. I want the exquisite texture and tone of the material to take center stage. Remember to choose carefully when using wallpaper, since fine examples can be very expensive to buy, put up (some wallpapers require professional installation), and take down.

LEARN FROM VERN

WHEN COLOR MEETS SURFACE

Ready to dip your roller and let rip with that beautiful pewter eggshell? Not so fast! Your paint is only as good as the surface it is on. Priming bare surfaces before painting is an important step when painting something for the first time. In older homes and fixers, you may find oil-based paint on the trim. If you try to apply latex over oil paint, you may be disappointed because it won't adhere properly. If you must paint latex over oil, sand the trim and use a primer specifically made to go from oil to latex.

An initial coat of primer also helps to seal the surface and hide slight irregularities. To help save on time and assist with coverage, primers can be tinted to match your eventual wall color. There are different primers for different surfaces, so ensure that you are using the right one for your surface. Many new paint products also include paint and primer in a combination that may save overall project time. Now that your surfaces have been primed, you really are ready to go.

LET IT SHINE

I often up the sheen factor in a dining room with a semi-gloss or luminescent paint finish; it's a formal space that can be more dramatic because it's not used every day or at least throughout the day, the way other public spaces in a house are. In addition, a high sheen paint finish allows the walls to bounce with candlelight, which simply makes the room feel more luxurious, special, and festive. Do be cautious and make sure your walls are in as good shape as possible with few, if any, imperfections because glossier paints highlight flaws.

WARM GREY IS A MODERN NEUTRAL

Warm Grey has been a dominant neutral color in design for several years now and continues to be popularly employed. It goes with every conceivable color, and its warm undertone tends to have a calm, organizing effect that's a nice counterbalance for the increasingly hectic lives that we all lead. Because Warm Grey is so accepting of other colors, painting your walls this color makes changing a room as easy as changing the accent colors in a space through throw pillows, art, and other decorative accessories. Cool Grey has also been heavily utilized but seems to be a little less adaptable to other colors and a little less welcoming, making it less easy to work with than its warmer cousin.

WARM AND COOL

Virtually every color has a warm version and a cooler version, depending on the undertone colors used to mix the paint. For instance, blue tones aren't necessarily always cool. There are many warm blues. Red isn't necessarily warm, some shades have very cool undertones. It all depends on the mix. In my New York and Atlanta homes, I use many colors people might say are cool, but I chose warm versions of the blues and grays that dominate in those properties.

PAINTING TRIM

In ceiling-challenged homes or homes with negligible trim details, and where it might be difficult to remove crown molding without a great deal of patching and repair, it often makes more sense to paint those elements the same color as the wall but in a semi- or high-gloss finish. For me, that's any space with ceiling heights less than 8 feet. By diminishing the contrast between the wall surface and the trim, you increase the perception of volume in a space. If you have fantastic-looking trim and plenty of volume, you may want to celebrate those elements by painting the trim in a color that contrasts with the wall surface (i.e., crisp white trim against a taupe or blue-grey wall).

EUROPE & AFRICA
ASIA & OCEANIA

LIVING SPACES:
FUNCTION, PERSONALITY & BEAUTY

Beautiful room arrangements don't simply create attractive rooms; they make people feel comfortable and welcome. The best arrangements emphasize what's good about a room by directing people toward special features and views, and minimize any negative features through the same clever placement. You can overcome most space imperfections with strategic planning.

ARRANGEMENT FUNDAMENTALS

- **Identify a focal point.** No matter what room you're putting together, always identify the main focal points in the space, and build seating areas around those focal points. Large windows offering a great view and fireplaces are two of the most common focal points in a space. If you're lucky to have one or both, create seating areas to take advantage of them.
- **Open it up.** Plan your furniture arrangement so that when you enter the room you immediately know where the seating areas are, and how to reach them. In other words, don't block the view or path in the room by placing a sofa in front of the entryway. The back of a sofa works like a visual wall, and prevents an easy flow through the space.
- **Layer it.** If your sofa is floating in the space, as opposed to sitting up against a wall, consider placing Place a sofa table, console, buffet, or other piece of long and low furniture behind it. This creates a more finished and more interesting look, offers more storage, and helps avoid the feeling of unintentionally walking "behind the scenes."
- **Don't block the view.** Never place the back of a sofa in front of a fireplace opening. Instead, consider a daybed, lounge, or pair of chairs that allow you to still visually connect with the glowing embers.
- **Get comfy.** Put the television in the room where you watch it, and make sure that there is ample comfortable seating facing it. Why make people (including you) crane their necks to watch a movie?
- **Island hop.** When deciding where to place an area rug, especially to punch out a conversational grouping (or groups) in a large space, make sure at least two front legs of all the seating furniture can sit on the rug comfortably—otherwise the rug might end up looking like it's floating without an anchor.
- **Go with the flow.** Always remember how people will navigate in and out of a room, and to and from seating areas. Give people at least 36″ for pathways between areas, and at least 24″ between pieces of furniture.

CRITICAL DISTANCES: FURNITURE PLACEMENT

We all want to be comfortable when sitting and enjoying a room—but we also have to get in and out of it with ease. Here are the numbers you need to know about arranging furniture:

- **18":** Distance between coffee table and sofa.
- **12":** Distance between lounge chair and dedicated ottoman.
- **24":** Distance between centerline of dining chairs.
- **24":** Minimum passage distance between furniture pieces.
- **36":** Ideal passage distance between furniture pieces and through a room.
- **12"** to **18":** Distance between rug edge and closest wall, fireplace hearth, or bump out.
- **2":** Minimum planning distance between furniture pieces or between furniture and wall
- **42"** to **120":** Minimum to maximum distance between seating pieces for ideal conversation.
- **26"** to **84":** Distance between primary seating and 1080p televisions 17" to 54" diagonal.

CHILDREN'S ROOMS:
FUNCTION, PERSONALITY & BEAUTY

Children's rooms should be built to last at least through the teen years—and with the right choices and a few design strategies, the fundamentals of these rooms can stand the test of time. Plan for the long term. A room that satiates an immediate need, or a short-term desire, will be obsolete within a few years.

When Craig and I brought our firstborn, Gavin, home, so many of our friends told us our lives would change forever. We'd have to put the crystal on high shelves, out of reach of little hands. Valuables would need to be hidden. Moreover, we'd never have an organized, tidy home again. Yet, I was raised in a household where I was surrounded by beautiful and precious things that I could touch and appreciate, and we try and raise our children the same way. We didn't move or change a thing in our houses, and both Vera and Gavin have grown up knowing and accepting what needs to be touched carefully versus what needs to be observed and not touched. They have learned to appreciate craftsmanship and what separates something that is ordinary from something that is a masterpiece. People can't believe it. "You can't possibly live like this or you don't really have kids and dogs," they say. But we do—we have five large dogs and two really active, happy kids. I've got living with kids and dogs figured out for our family, yet I understand every family is different and has specific needs.

Both Craig and I are really busy, like any other working couple. We help each other in our businesses and are involved with each other professionally. It's absolutely necessary that we have a life where things are organized; otherwise life at home would be complete and utter chaos. We simply don't have time to organize the house over and over again. By putting the right pieces in the right places that allow for ease of organization, and by using the right kinds of durable, forgiving materials, we are able to keep the house in order. It is easier to maintain a sense of order when you have the right kinds of storage. Another benefit is the peace it brings everyone. When you arrive home from a busy and tiring day, you are rejuvenated instead of daunted by the mess that greets you. And while the kids have indeed broken a piece or two, it's a rare occurrence, and certainly not a tragedy. I believe they are developing an aesthetic sense and an appreciation for nice things. Of course, I can't speak for our dogs in this regard—but they *are* well behaved!

- **Avoid themed rooms if possible.** Your kids might love a particular cartoon character today, but tomorrow it could be another. Instead of investing in licensed character wallpapers and expensive bedding, choose affordable, replaceable decorative items like pillows and lamps.
- **Avoid too many bright colors:** It's tempting to use bright colors as the foundation for kids' rooms, but their appeal often fades much faster than they do. Keep in mind that kids' toys are often very colorful and stimulating. When they co-exist in a room that's also super stimulating, it can be hard to know where to focus in my opinion. A calming or neutral shell is the perfect backdrop for all of that colorful stuff.

- **Establish a long-term foundation:** Choose wall colors, drapery, and rugs that can easily adapt to changing tastes. Think of them as a subtle backdrop for accessories that can modify the look of the room with the seasons or evolving tastes. This is, of course, valid advice even for grown-up rooms.

- **Involve children:** Of course, a child's room should be a collaborative effort. So, if your child wants purple or some other bright color in their room, don't shut down that conversation. My daughter's favorite colors are orange and red, so we talked about how we could incorporate orange into her room without painting the walls. Here's a fun test you can give your kids when it comes to color: if you look at a color and then shut your eyes and the color still appears, it's too intense for their walls!

- **Have fun inside the closet:** Instead of painting a kid's room bright orange, pink, yellow, or blue, use that super-stimulating color inside their closets! Those kinds of colors are livable long term when they're not in your face all the time. And having them in your closet makes opening the closet fun! And just maybe the kids will hang up their clothes.

- **Pick a great pendant or ceiling feature:** Kids spend a lot of time staring at their ceilings, so give them something interesting and stimulating to look at. A well-designed and interesting light fixture or ceiling medallion are great options. Consider painting the ceiling pale blue to mimic the sky, but hold back from painting clouds. The more literal a feature, the shorter its lifespan.

- **Put a dimmer on wall switches:** Dimming the lights to help create the right mood in kids' rooms is a worthwhile investment. Lighting is just as important in children's spaces as it is in public and grown-up spaces. Light control allows you to create a calming atmosphere or a stimulating one—whatever is right for the situation.

- **Buy most furniture from the adult section:** Buy a changing tray to sit on top of a dresser that will last long after they're out of diapers, instead of a nursery changing table that you'll have to sell or dispose of after they're potty trained. The same can be said for gliders or rockers: pick one that visually translates into a great reading chair once they're old enough to use them, instead of one with exaggerated proportions covered in pastels.

- **Get a bigger bed:** If you have the room, consider putting them in a full or queen-size bed, instead of a twin, once it's safe enough for them to switch out of a crib or toddler bed. It might not be right for everyone, but if your child is comfortable in a full or queen-size bed, they'll potentially be in that bed for as long as they're in your house. They may even be able to take it with them when they move into their own home.

- **Choose art and accessories that they'll grow to appreciate:** Kids spend a lot of time in their rooms, so it's worthwhile to outfit them with elements that will pique their curiosity while their brains are still so malleable. In my opinion, it's never too early to expose kids to great design and art. They'll stand a better chance of becoming adults who are visually sensitive to the fundamentals of good design: proportion, balance, and scale.

- **Purchase closed storage:** Bookshelves are great for books, but I'm wary of too many open storage pieces with exposed shelves for other items such as toys and other collectibles. Messy! If you do have exposed shelves, look for solid bins that provide plenty of useful and accessible storage to make putting away their toys easy for all. Solid doors and drawers are great for keeping a room neat and clean.

PLAYBILL
THE BARRYMORE THEATRE
THE CURIOUS INCIDENT OF THE DOG IN THE NIGHT-TIME
PLAYBILL
BELASCO THEATRE
HEDWIG
NGRY INCH
OM WITH A VIEW

ART & ACCESSORIES:
FUNCTION, PERSONALITY & BEAUTY

I always say that the best invitation is the invitation to a home filled with pieces that are meaningful to the owners and that tell their story. Accessories are a wonderful and special way to tell a story on a more intimate level. Each person and each journey is unique, and homes should reflect the multi-dimensionality of people, their families, and their experiences. It won't happen overnight, but the goal should be to accessorize your home with items that build a narrative about you and your family. These don't have to be expensive items; they just have to be meaningful and pleasant for you to look at.

A PLACE FOR EVERYTHING

- **Bases and Plinths:** Properly showcasing your beloved accessories and treasures by placing them on bases, plinths, and in display boxes will elevate them, both literally and figuratively. Almost no one notices these supporting accessories, but bases and plinths can take something a little under-scaled or insignificant, and add distinction and visual value to it by literally lifting it closer to the sight line. A plinth gives you a chance to remove an item from the visual clutter of the supporting surface. I usually like simple, black wood or clear glass bases and plinths and have had them made when I can't find pre-made ones large enough. They're not meant to be noticed, so having them in a bright color or with intricate detailing would take away the attention from the object and bring it to the base. It's the equivalent of an overly ornate frame that then distracts from the beauty of the art itself. Simple pedestal bases are also good for elevating sculptures and larger accessories.

- **Display Boxes:** Display boxes and cases have become popular lately, too. They're a great way to group disparate objects and present them cohesively while protecting them from dust. Once something is in a box or case, it not only feels more important, but it also makes it feel larger and more purposeful. Think of how museums display their precious items. Almost everything that's not hanging on a wall is on a base, plinth, pedestal, and/or in a display case. This calls attention to these objects and elevates their presence and importance in a room.

- **Size Matters:** I've always said that it's better to have fewer, larger-scaled items than it is to have many, small-scaled items. Although they can be beautiful and precious, small accessories tend to litter the visual landscape . . . especially when they're numerous and placed together without purpose. Most of us tend to under-scale our accessories for fear of something feeling too big in a space. For me, it's always better to make a strong statement with a single, large personality piece than it is to not say much with several easy-to-accommodate, portable small pieces. If you want to display small pieces, create a logical collection and place them on a single base or inside a display box. Several small pieces grouped together and presented correctly can have the statement-making power of a single, large accessory.

Vietnamese Ceramics: A Separate Trad
ULTIMATE TROPICAL

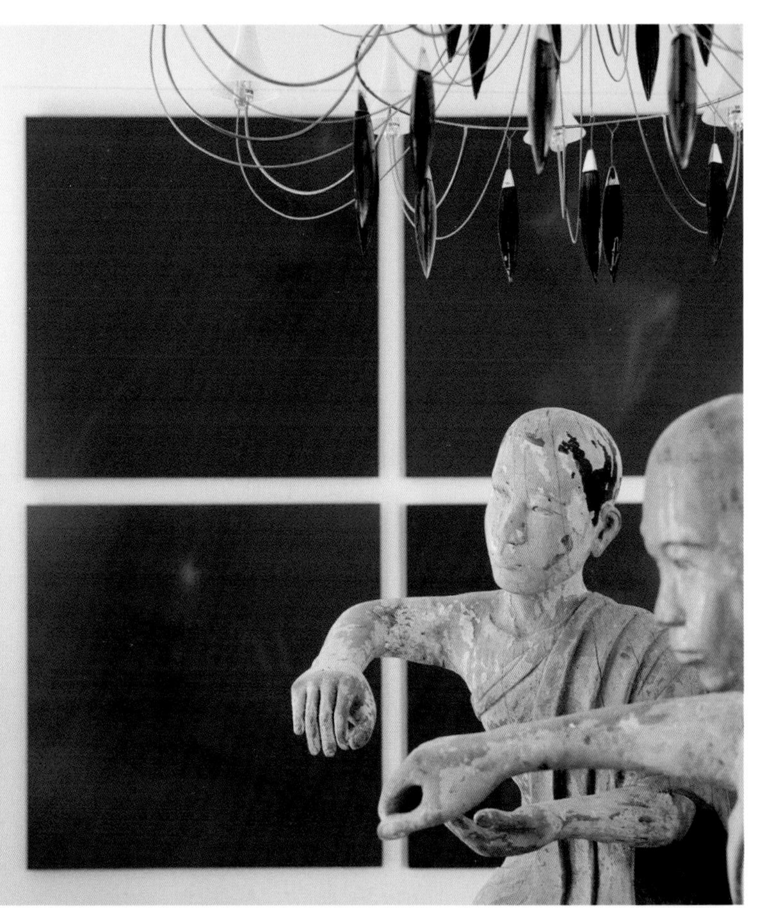

IGGY PECK ARCHITECT

AND EVERYTHING IN ITS PLACE

- **Mix Styles in Adjacencies:** Items always shine brighter when they're adjacent to an opposite. I love the adjacencies of rough against smooth, metal next to wood, textured alongside highly polished, intricately detailed on top of completely plain, and brightly colored in conjunction with an expanse of neutral. When there's too much of one thing in one place, the beauty of that item can be difficult to appreciate fully. It needs its opposite to optimally shine.

- **Boxes:** I'm a big fan of boxes substantial enough to store unattractive, utilitarian (but necessary) objects and for organizing the day-to-day clutter of life. Boxes are decorative accessories that are both functional and visually pleasing. They are made almost everywhere, with a wide range of detail and color, so they're one of my favorite things to pick up on travels. I always take critical measurements of items like remotes, tablets, the largest magazines I peruse, and other items that I might want visually out of the way. When I purchase a box, it needs to be substantial enough to do the job I need it to. Because boxes are generally clean-lined in shape, they don't create additional visual clutter when they're sitting on a coffee table, nightstand, or entry foyer table.

- **Handcrafted, Vintage, and Antique Items:** Items with history have a way of lending soul to new spaces. When homes are filled with all-new items, they can feel flat and two-dimensional, even if they're perfectly space planned and full of expensive goods. These kinds of rooms often feel one-note and without a story to tell. Unfortunately, as technology becomes a more dominant part of cultures around the globe, there are fewer artisans who possess the skills and techniques to create masterfully handcrafted items that showcase the history of a country, region, culture, or group of people. Finely executed handmade items are largely a thing of the past.

- **Hangers:** One of the easiest updates you can do in your closet is hang clothing on matching hangers. It may be one of the few times I advise matching like items in a room. You will be amazed at what a difference it makes in terms of aesthetics. I prefer the sturdiness of wooden hangers so I buy packages of 8 from IKEA for less than $5. They come in natural, black, or white, so you can choose the tone you want.

- **Meaning:** When you pass by, pick up, or look at the accessories and art in your home, they should serve as fond reminders of your journey through life. Getting to this point is not easy. Everyone necessarily fills his or her home with placeholder accessories to help occupy some of the temporary emptiness of a new home or a fresh start. Even if you can't immediately fill your home with special and meaningful treasures, take your time in selecting things that you genuinely love and eventually replace less meaningful items with ones that you acquire on trips, as gifts, or on fun-filled treasure hunts.

- **Quality Counts:** Although I love to include items from my travels, these items don't have to be exotic or from far-flung lands to be effective. Anything that's been made with skill, or has an interesting patina or texture brought on by the passage of time, can help imbue a room with feeling. You can also look to items that have been passed on from generation to generation in your family and think of unique ways to display them. The idea here is to mix in items with detail, patina, and character alongside newly acquired goods so that your home feels thoughtful and uniquely yours.

Sotheby's
TRADITIONAL HOME
ROSEMARY BEACH
Arts of Ancient Viet Nam

LOUIS SULLIVAN
MARRAKESH BY DESIGN
Classic Thai
Chiang Mai Style
I BELIEVE IN ZERO
BAZAAR
domino
KELLY HOPPEN
EAST MEETS WEST
KELLY HOPPEN HOME
Monochrome Home
KELLY HOPPEN STYLE
ROBERT A.M. STERN HOUSES AND GARDENS
SO CHIC
STYLE AND SUBSTANCE
les must de Cartier
Let's Get Comfortable
Spanish Style
Perfect Neutrals
PROVENCE THE ART OF LIVING
TULSA ART DECO
The Garden Book
AXEL VERVOORDT
New Seaside Interiors
Paris Interiors
Remodelista
THE HEIGHT OF STYLE
WANAKA
Arnold Newman

- **Framing:** When framing art, I recommend using white or off-white matting. Colored mats detract from the art, while white or off-white lets it shine. Matting comes in two thicknesses, 4-ply and 8-ply. The first is the most common, as 8-ply is more expensive. I think 8-ply is worth paying extra for because it elevates the artwork within the mat and gives it presence. Be sure to ask for acid-free matting if you are framing a valuable or important piece that you want to protect.

- **All glass is not created equal:** Select the right glass for your framed piece and keep in mind that there is tremendous difference in price between glass types. The glass in many off-the-rack, inexpensive frames may not have UV protection, so always know what you are buying. UV glass eliminates many of the harmful effects of the sun. Museum glass eliminates both sun damage and glare.

- **Place art in unexpected places:** Framed artwork (with protective glass over it) makes a huge difference to the feel of kitchen and bathrooms spaces, and there's no reason why you shouldn't inject color, fun, and style into these functional spots. Do be careful about placing any artwork that might get damaged by heat too close to a cooking appliance. Protective glass should keep your artwork from getting damaged by water from a nearby sink, but be careful about high humidity, which can impact framed and unframed pieces alike. Avoid putting anything irreplaceable or highly prized in these areas, just in case! Posters, maps, photographs, vintage menus, and lithographs are all appropriate choices as long as they are not extremely valuable or irreplaceable to you.

- **Books and Magazines:** Well-worn novels, beautiful art books, and antiquarian volumes transform a house into a home. Books are visual and textual elements that also happen to engage people. Every room in the house can benefit from the life and soul physical books add to a space.

  » Instead of just relegating books to bookshelves, place them on side tables, coffee tables, and nightstands as well. I like large groupings of books throughout the house, distributed by subjects such as travel, design, art, cooking, and fiction.

  » Neat stacks of current magazines can also be found throughout my house. Keeping organized stacks of books, progressing from largest on the bottom to smallest at the top, prevents rooms from feeling disheveled and overrun by reading material.

  » My preference is for bookshelves to hold horizontal stacks of books in lieu of vertically organizing them. Whether you place your books this way or in the traditional vertical fashion, implement some kind of organization of subject matter, followed by stacking from tallest to shortest with spines pulled forward to even out depth differences.

  » Mix decorative items onto bookshelves, whether they're stacked horizontally or vertically, to prevent shelves from feeling flat, solely functional, and one-dimensional. Whenever possible, I try to purchase the hardcover copy of a book. Aside from the fact that they are more durable than soft cover books, I generally find hard bound books much easier to display and integrate into the décor of my rooms.

- **Candlesticks & Candles:** Although most of my work is only experienced visually, I have always felt that scent and candlelight are important components when styling a room. The most beautiful and well-done room is difficult to appreciate if it smells bad, so having a pleasant-smelling candle or fragrance warmer is a must for completing any room that I live in or work on. Candles add irreplaceable ambiance and life to a space, even when they're not lit. The look of tapers or pillars, on candlesticks, in lanterns, or on candle trays, helps tell the story of a room. For me, nothing can replace the flicker of a real candle flame when trying to create a warm, romantic, and inviting environment.

VOGUE LIVING HOUSES GARDENS PEOPLE
The Hotel Book
Wild Romance

EASY SEASONAL CHANGES

Changing one or two large decorative accessories seasonally in a room can be a fun way to keep your rooms feeling fresh and interesting. We become accustomed to what we see every day, and over time we stop noticing the beauty of our things, unless we occasionally move things around. To successfully freshen up interiors seasonally, ensure that the vast majority of your rooms' foundational items are neutral. Wall paint, upholstery, and rugs are all considered foundation items of a space. When these pieces are neutral, they give you a base to build upon. Although it may not be feasible or even desirable to change up the majority of the accessories in a room, changing out one or two major pieces each season is generally very doable. Focus on statement pieces that have visual impact and that are placed in prominent locations within a room to get the most bang for your effort. Here are some of the easiest and most inexpensive ways to change the appearance of your room:

- **Decorative Pillows:** Pillows can really change up the look of large items like your upholstery pieces and bed. If you're lacking storage for full pillow cover and insert change outs, stick to your insert sizes and change out the pillow covers only. Pillow covers, when empty, fold flat to take up minimal space.
- **Top of Bed:** Your bed is likely the largest piece of furniture real estate in your home, so what's on it has a powerful impact on the visuals of your space. We spend about a third of our lives in bed, so make sure you love what you see and are comfortable sleeping with it. Changing up the duvet (or comforter), shams, decorative pillows, and sheets is a quick and easy way to give your bedroom a seasonal makeover. Make sure that your seasonal options all work with the elements in your bedroom that will remain static, like your rug, wall color, drapery, and other large upholstered pieces.
- **Home Fragrance:** I change scents with the season. For me a scent helps a room feel different, even if I don't change anything else. In spring, I use a fresh citrus scent, in summer lemongrass mint, and in fall I use a five spice or similar scent. In winter, I love sandelwood.
- **Throws:** Coordinate changing out your throw with changing out your decorative pillows for a more complete and directed change. Also, think about the different weights of throws available. You may want a lighter weight throw in a brighter color out in the middle of summer and a darker, richer, and heavier throw out in the winter.
- **Organic Elements:** I love changing the organic elements in rooms to reflect the current season's color palette. In summer and fall, I might showcase Golden Delicious apples in the spring and summer, bright green Granny Smith apples in the fall, and Red Delicious for winter. The same can be said for the color palette of my orchids and cut flowers. By shifting their colors with the seasons, you subtly change the overall mood and tone of your rooms.
- **Accessories:** Not everything you own has to be out at the same time. You certainly wouldn't wear every piece of jewelry you own at the same time, why is it any different for home décor? Rotating accessories is a wonderful way to truly appreciate all of the beautiful things you've accumulated over the years. For instance, I like to change my side and coffee tables according to the seasons (shells in a glass dish in summer; vintage ornaments and candlesticks during winter holidays).

COLLECTIONS:
FUNCTION, PERSONALITY & BEAUTY

To be honest, I have more stuff than is necessary to function, but what I have is meaningful to me. My things are well made, but more importantly, they are filled with my history and the history of my culture, my experiences, my mother, my family, and my travels. I may not see them every day, but I still want these mementos to be there. When I'm home, I want to feel I am ensconced by things that remind me of my journey. As a result, my houses are uniquely customized to my family and me. Your home should be that way, too. Collections are such an important part of tailoring a home to fit your personality, but we're sometimes unsure of how to best enjoy them, and it's easy to get overwhelmed.

This was really brought home to me during an assignment on *Trading Spaces*. I was tasked with redoing a very small master bedroom in a romantic way. The wife had a very large collection of snow globes, and the husband had an impressive group of bobble head baseball sports figures. They were stored in the bedroom, and the couple wanted to keep them there. Snow globes and bobble heads don't exactly spell romance, however, so I had to come up with a way to deal with them because I wanted the couple to be happy.

The solution was to build wall-to-wall storage units. This left plenty of room for the couple to circulate around what was a fairly small bedroom. Since neither collection required a lot of depth, we were able to create shallow shelves behind thin doors with open shelves above. That way, 80 percent of their collections were behind the doors, and 20 percent were on display on the open shelving. Husband and wife could change or rotate the collection according to seasons, holidays, or simply their whim. The predominantly closed storage solution gave the couple a chance to truly enjoy their collections, by allowing them to focus their attention on a limited number of pieces throughout the year. Of course, it helped hide most of it in order to create a more romantic setting, which was my goal for the room.

If you have a large collection, whether it's of bobble heads, rolling pins, or coffee mugs, find a closed storage solution for most of the items, and display a limited number of examples in an attractive grouping either on a shelf, on the wall, or any other surface that allows you to enjoy these special pieces. Like my couple, rotate your collection on a regular basis to breathe new life and interest into your display.

LEARN FROM VERN

GO GLOBAL

If there is one element that defines "Vern Yip style," it is my preference for clean lines, whether that is translated into modern, contemporary, traditional, or something in between. Ethnic pieces mixed in bring a great deal of personality to these streamlined, modern rooms. Indigenous artifacts are by nature timeless; anything that references a particular cultural tradition is enduring. Every room in my house has artifacts from dozens of countries we've visited, and they coexist quite nicely with my modern aesthetic. For instance, in my foyer, architectural relics from a Thai temple are juxtaposed with a modern Baccarat chandelier, statues of monks from Myanmar, and a Vietnamese painting. I surround myself with my life experiences in this way.

LAYERED PATTERNS

Like color, pattern is an important way to tell your individual story and make your home uniquely yours. Mixing patterns within a single color palette is a sophisticated and rewarding way to create unique and varied visual interest that still feels pulled together. The key to successfully layering patterns is to ensure that you employ a mix of pattern scales to include small, medium, large, and extra-large. Sticking to just one scale of pattern can overwhelm or underwhelm a room, making it feel visually uncomfortable to inhabit, since the eye doesn't have a directed progression from one place to the next. Along with varying the pattern scale, include a mix of pattern types, such as geometrics, stripes, and organics, for a more balanced visual. Solids can then assist with providing visual relief and support.

EDIT

When recreating a space, consider moving some pieces to a different room. Editing is one of the most powerful tools you have, and it is free. You can sell or give things away that no longer serve your purposes, or you can use a piece in a whole new way in an entirely different room. A dining room buffet becomes a sofa table, an office credenza, or storage in a bedroom. A rug that no longer works in the living room might be perfect in a bedroom; a small bookshelf that's wrong in the bedroom might be perfect to hold towels in the bathroom. Once weeded out and scaled down, your best-loved items can shine in a new way—and you have a better idea of what you might need to add back in. Additionally, consider shifting art and furniture from one space to another. Your eyes get accustomed to seeing things where they've been, and you lose the appreciation that originally drew you to the artwork to begin with.

THE BEST OF DESIGNERS' CHALLENGE
ROMANTIC STYLE
classic style
INSIDE OUT

FLOWERS & ORGANICS:
FUNCTION, PERSONALITY & BEAUTY

Organic items are critical toward making a house feel like a true home. Not everyone has a green thumb, the time to properly care for real organic items, or the right light conditions, but a home without organics is barren and incomplete. Since I travel so much for work and lead such a busy family and professional life, here are some tricks that work for me:

- **Fresh Fruit:** A glass cylinder filled with citrus similarly adds color, texture, and the natural world to the great indoors. It's so simple, clean, fresh, and modern—but also works with any décor. Large bowls of apples is something that I've done for years and continue to love to do to this day. A pre-packaged bag of five or six Granny Smith or Red Delicious apples can often be had for three to four dollars—sometimes less. I will put several bags in a large bowl and set it on a coffee table or side table for décor. The apples eventually start to discolor and go bad after a couple of weeks, so warn your guests and family not to eat them if they are just out for display. For less than $10, you have a gorgeous organic statement that requires no maintenance and adds a bright, fresh pop of color to any space. Alternatively, enjoy them as an edible item that doubles as décor.

- **Cut Flowers:** I love having fresh, cut flowers in the house and have them regularly when possible. Depending on how big your place is or how busy you are, having fresh flowers distributed throughout your house is not always feasible, however. My advice is invest in long-lasting blossoms, such as Gerbera daisies, hydrangea, and roses, and add them to décor on special occasions, or when you feel the need for a special treat. What I *don't* recommend is pretending that silk or plastic plants are a good substitute for the real thing. For me, their color and shape is a little too consistent with flowers and leaves that lack sufficient natural variation. Their inexpensive look brings down the entire level of the room.

- **Orchid Plants:** Many feel that orchids have been overdone, but I'm a real fan of their beautiful architectural look, incredible value, and ease of maintenance. Orchids look expensive and hard to maintain, but they are very affordable, and it takes some effort to kill them. Sometimes I feel that mine do better with less attention. Placed in bright, indirect sunlight and watered every ten days to two weeks, an orchid plant can produce spectacular, real blooms that last for up to eight weeks. I've had very high quality specimens last even longer. Widely available at grocery stores and home improvement centers in addition to nurseries and florists, orchid plants can be had for under $20, depending on the marketplace and season. This is a bargain for beautiful flowers that can last nearly two months.

  Choose a specimen with several buds still left to open. I usually select one with two or three open flowers with at least four or five buds left to go. A fully bloomed version looks spectacular in the store but won't last you nearly as long. Orchid plants are air plants, so it's important that you don't transplant them into soil. If you don't like the decorative pot that it comes in, keep the orchid in its nursery pot, place it in a larger decorative pot that's more to your taste, make it snug with Styrofoam peanuts stuffed into the gaps between the two, and cover the top with a layer of sheet moss. My favorite orchids are the commonly found white Phalaenopsis (otherwise known as the moth orchid), but I also like the harder-to-find Sharry Baby, which has numerous small, pink and dark red blooms that smell like chocolate.

- **Preserved Boxwood Topiaries:** More widely available than they used to be, preserved boxwoods are most commonly offered in architectural, sculpted ball, cone, and spiral topiaries. Although they can be expensive, the boxwood leaves on these specimens are real but have been chemically preserved to last for years with minimal maintenance, no sunlight, and no watering aside from an occasional light misting. So it is a worthy investment. I also love that their tailored shapes aren't trying to fool anyone into thinking that they're real, living plants. They fill a gap somewhere between a houseplant and an accessory. The leaves look incredibly real because they *are* real and have the natural variation in shape that you'd find on live boxwood. For me, they're the perfect way to add something that's easy maintenance, organic, and architectural simultaneously.
- **Preserved Roses:** Preserved roses appeared several years ago, and I find them to be a great solution for building a foundation of no-maintenance organics around the house. There is variation in each rose, just as there is in nature, because these were at one time live roses. No two are identical. Each has been chemically preserved and are available dyed in a variety of mostly natural-looking colors. I personally gravitate towards the whites, oranges, reds, and yellows, which look the most natural to me. Unlike fresh, cut flower arrangements, I never need to change the water or re-cut stems. The initial investment may be steeper than purchasing the real thing, and they certainly don't have the lovely scent of real flowers, but they're beautifully natural in appearance and significantly cheaper over the long run.

FLORAL ARRANGEMENTS

Whether it's a bunch of wild daisies dancing casually in a mason jar, or an elaborate formal creation, a floral arrangement can be a finishing touch that adds warmth, color, and joy to the dining table, kitchen island, or coffee table—wherever you need a splash of color. If you plan on placing arrangements in the middle of a dining table as a centerpiece, don't go higher than 15 inches, otherwise the view across the table will be obstructed. That said, assembling your own centerpieces is an opportunity to express your artistic sensibilities, and I encourage you to experiment with the color, shape, size, and combinations of the blossoms you choose. Indeed, flower arranging is an art that you can spend years studying, but never tire of. However, I caution against trying to make very elaborate arrangements on your own. Sometimes, such arrangements don't turn out as spectacularly as you had hoped and, for that reason, are best left to the pros. However, here are the fundamentals that will get you started on simple and lovely center or feature floral arrangements.

SELECT THE FLOWERS

- White or pale-hued flowers often look best in brighter vases that balance the overall look of the arrangement.
- Keep the height of the vase and flowers combined to 15 inches or less if used as a centerpiece for a sit down meal. This allows most guests to see across the table and converse without a visual obstruction.
- Bold or brightly colored flowers are best in clear, neutral, or pale-hued vases that allow them to shine without competition.
- For arrangements near food, avoid flowers with a strong or overpowering fragrance that will compete with scents from your food.

Choose the Right Vase

Flowers	Bud	Cube	Cylinder	Sphere	Rectangle	Trumpet
Birds of Paradise		•	•		•	•
Calla Lilies		•	•		•	•
Carnations	•	•	•	•		•
Daisies	•	•	•	•		•
Gerbera Daisies	•	•	•	•		•
Gladioli		•	•		•	•
Hydrangea		•	•	•		•
Large-leaf Greens	•	•	•	•	•	•
Lilies		•	•		•	•
Long-Stem Roses	•	•	•	•	•	•
Mums	•	•	•			•
Orchids	•	•	•		•	•
Peonies	•	•		•		•
Sunflowers		•	•		•	
Sweetheart Roses	•	•		•		•
Thin-leaf Greens	•	•		•	•	•
Tulips	•	•	•	•		•

WORLD ATLAS AND ENCYCLOPEDIA
Planet Earth AN ILLUSTRATED HISTORY

ZEN
ARCHITECTURE TODAY

Vietnamese Ceramics: A Separate Tradition
ULTIMATE TROPICAL

DESIGN AND MAINTAIN THE ARRANGEMENT

- Flower stems should be no longer than 1.5 times the vase height; otherwise you arrangement will look top heavy.
- Clear or translucent vases require you to remove leaves from each stem and, potentially, dress the inside with something decorative.
- Glass vases should have a one-eighth inch or greater lip to ensure that they don't break or chip easily.
- Cut stems at an angle under running water or below water to prevent clogging by air bubbles. The angle maximizes the stem surface taking in water, and by cutting in water, you encourage hydration, allowing water to travel throughout successfully, thus prolonging the life of the flower.
- For large mouth vases, create a floral tape grid onto the mouth of the vase, or fill the bottom with pebbles or stones to help keep flowers where you want them.
- Create a flower dome by starting with a central flower in your hand. Keep adding all the way around, spiraling the stems out for a no-fail end product. A clear rubber band can help keep the converging stems in place. This type of arrangement is best suited to a spherical vase.
- Re-cut stems every two to three days to ensure a clean and fresh cut that will maximize flower freshness.
- Change water daily for best results. Life-shortening bacteria can grow in water that's been sitting too long.

LEARN FROM VERN

NOT YOUR MOTHER'S CENTERPIECE

Most people think of a centerpiece as flowers, arranged formally in a vessel and placed in the middle of the table. Flowers are fabulous, of course, but consider opening yourself up to other possibilities when thinking about table decoration. There are so many natural and artistic objects that make dramatic and lovely centerpieces. Organic materials other than flowers are lovely. For instance, a bowl of beautiful green apples or lemons is an easy, fool-proof spring or summer centerpiece; a compote filled with small gourds and pumpkins is nice in fall. Sculptural twigs or architectural leaves can be dramatic any time of year. As with a floral centerpiece, keep the height to 15 inches or less.

Aside from fruit, other kinds of food can make for spectacular focal points on a table. For instance, if you have a phenomenal cake, why wait until dessert to show it off? Cakes are actually the perfect centerpiece, since they are generally lower than 15 inches—the best height for conversation across a table. I have built table settings around one spectacular cake on a pedestal, anchored by small vases of flowers around it. One year, a wonderful German bakery made us an incredible yule log cake or *bûche de Noël.* It was exquisite, adorned with marzipan squirrels, twigs, and leaves—so many marvelous details. I felt it should be prominently displayed for all to enjoy. What better place than the middle of the dining table? Another terrific baker we know, Tina at Sweet Henrietta's in Florida, makes a special white-on-white cake for us. She covers it in swirls of white frosting and then adorns the top with white chocolate seashells, starfish, and seahorses that she molds herself. We put that out as the centerpiece and build the table setting around it. Another plus of putting a cake in the middle of table: guests leave room for dessert if they see it, so they pace themselves at dinner.

How about a beautiful grouping of candles in various heights and widths? Make sure to avoid scented candles in a dining situation (it competes with the aromas of the food). Use your imagination and make the centerpiece something that reflects the event, your guests, or yourself. For example, ask your guests to name their favorite book. Get copies of those books and stack and arrange them artfully in the middle of the table. This is an icebreaker and a conversation starter because everyone has their book on the table; it's something to talk about. Try something similar with framed photographs and family snapshots. Everyone can submit a favorite photo. Frame them and place them in an interesting fashion down the center of the table. That way, everyone can see a photo or two and talk about the memories they evoke during dinner.

A centerpiece doesn't have to be in the middle of a table to be a focal point. Many people feel the real estate in the center of a table is too valuable, as it's needed for serving platters. If you have a rectangular or oval table, the centerpiece—now called an endpiece!—can be placed at either end. I do this often in New York City, where our table abuts a window. We place flowers and candles or other adornments on that end of the table. Since this means we aren't limited by the 15-inch rule, we can go as tall and dramatic as we like with our table décor. When adding decoration to the end of a table, experiment with height, because whatever you choose, whether a tall vase or even a sculpture, it won't obstruct the view across the table.

OUTDOOR LIVING:

FUNCTION, PERSONALITY & BEAUTY

As you learned when you went shopping for outdoor furniture, more now so than ever, outdoor furniture offers the same level of function and comfort as indoor furniture provides. Better yet, advancements in materials make it possible to design your outdoor rooms as true extensions of your interior spaces. Arranging an outdoor room is similar to creating an indoor furniture arrangement, with a few caveats:

- Identify your main focal points in the space, and build seating areas around those focal points. For instance, place seating and dining areas to take in broad vistas and other beautiful views, such as natural water features, mountain views, or an interesting perspective on gardens, flowerbeds, and borders.
- When placing furniture on a patio or deck adjacent to interior spaces and open spaces, place furniture in such a way that it does not impede "indoor outdoor" living—in other words, you want to be able to easily go from indoors to outside without having to navigate around obstacles. Moreover, you want the same easement from patio, porch, or deck to green spaces, grass areas, and gardens that lie beyond the living areas.
- A fireplace or fire pit can become its own cozy and separate seating area, away from areas closer to interior spaces. When placing chairs, a minimum of 3 to 5 feet from the edge of the fire pit is required for safety and comfort. An area of about 15 x 15 feet is adequate for placing 4 to 6 chairs around a fire pit of 5 feet in diameter.
- Use the same Critical Distances for placing indoor furniture (page 15) for your outdoor arrangements.

PART TWO:

A SENSE OF PLACE

Location plays an important part in style choices. In the following chapters, I open the doors of each of my homes to demonstrate—through full-room shots and intimate vignettes and details—how the rules of design, a sense of place, and personal taste help inform my choices. Part Two is essentially Part One in action. Now you'll discover specifically how the principles explored in the previous section work in "real life" in my own homes. Even though each of my three homes are different styles, and have different décor, I have applied the rules in this book to all of them. For example, my drapes are always hung as close to the ceiling as possible; my sofas and coffee tables are 18" apart; and my hanging fixtures are 66" from the finished floor to the lowest point of the fixture when hung over my dining room tables. These rules free me up to focus on choosing colors, fabrics, textures, and forms. The fun part!

Each home covers, in a unique way, three of the big design "archetypes": traditional, urban, and waterfront. More importantly, you can see very clearly through these beautiful photographs how I combine my background in architecture, design, business, and science with the practical needs of my family to create homes that provide both what we want and what we need.

AROUND THE WORLD IN 125 YEARS
EUROPE & AFRICA
AROUND THE WORLD IN 125 YEARS
ASIA & OCEANIA

CHAPTER FOUR:
SOUTHERN COMFORT

Before Craig and I bought our 1925 home in Atlanta we had driven by it many times. Even before meeting, and long before it was even on the market, we each had independently come to the conclusion that it looked like the perfect place to someday raise a family. Situated prominently on a hill and replete with a flat back yard, it was easy to envision our future kids playing there and our family someday becoming a part of this charming and safe neighborhood. When we finally noticed a For Sale sign on the house, we couldn't call the real estate agent fast enough. Negotiations immediately escalated into a bidding war—and we lost to a developer. The house sits on a double lot and there was talk of tearing it down to accommodate two new, more valuable homes.

So we were devastated that we had lost the house of our dreams. A very nice doctor and his wife had lived there for 26 years, raising their three boys to adulthood. They were only the third family to live in the house, which had a long, consistent history of being a great place to raise kids. And we had lost it. But in a huge stroke of luck, the house came back to us. Knowing we would maintain the property as a place where children would grow, play, and enjoy the community, they miraculously accepted our lower offer and we have gratefully raised our family there ever since.

The house has incredible energy, its southern exposure and architecture allows for a lot of natural light in almost every room. I refer to the house as a "reverse shotgun" in that it has a very wide elevation, but it's not very deep. That means most rooms benefit from the natural light the southern exposure guarantees. The double lot is very private and quite lush. In fact we have the Georgia State Champion elm tree in our backyard.

I love the character of homes built before the 1930's with their wavy glass windowpanes, imperfect wood floors, and unique architectural detailing. However, the house did need some updates. To the surprise of my contractor, I outlined a remodel schedule of ten days. Being on television for over fifteen years, I'm used to an accelerated and ambitious timeline. I recall once building and furnishing a three-story brick house from the ground up in a little over a week, including the landscaping, for a television pilot. I know how to layer sub-contractors and run a job site. Ripping up worn wall-to-wall carpet, refinishing hardwood floors, stripping wallpaper, and giving the entire interior a fresh coat of paint were just the initial steps. We also gave the house a much-needed prominent front door and foyer by enclosing a deep, front facing screened-in porch. In the following years, we took more time to add on to the house, which had already set precedent with another addition built in the 1940s. Developing and testing new products, shooting television shows, and serving as a setting for magazine and book spreads are just a few of the activities that happen here on a daily basis. And since so many of my fans and customers lead busy lives similar to ours (filled with hectic schedules, kids, and dogs), we have the perfect product test conditions already in place!

Today, when I walk in the door, I have a huge smile on my face. When I am in that environment, I feel happy, stimulated, and surrounded by the people, objects, and memories I love. The most gratifying compliment I hear from visitors is that while the house looks quite grand from the outside it feels like a warm family home inside. That was our goal. The house itself feels very right to me. That is what I wish for you. The whole purpose of this book is to help you create the kind of environment that makes you feel whole . . . and at home.

EUROPE & AFRICA
TASCHEN
ASIA & OCEANIA
TASCHEN

NEW YORK
NEW YORK

LUXURY HOTELS
LUXURY FOR DOGS

THAILAND
BOUCHON • BAKERY
SLOW COOKING
GRILLING
THE MR. FOOD COOKBOOK
JEAN-GEORGES
PASTRIES
A BOAT, A WHALE & A WALRUS

Zeynep Fadıllıoğlu
LIVING ARCHITECTURE
1000 c DEYROLLE
I SPEAK OF AFRICA
THE LEOPARDS
LEX HES
An illustrated book of Burmese Court Textiles
ALEXANDER McQUEEN EVOLUTION
RUUD VAN EMPEL
VOGUE LIVING HOUSES, GARDENS, PEOPLE
ALEXANDER McQUEEN: SAVAGE BEAUTY
VEE SPEERS
bulletproof
The Hotel Book
Wild Romance

Versailles – Garden of Statues
HERSCHER
ARA GÜLER's Istanbul
SOUTH
THE MALE NUDES
Fault Lines/Turkey/East/West
The New Acropolis Museum
EMERALD CITIES ARTS OF SIAM AND BURMA, 1775-1950
MARRAKECH

Sotheby's
PHOTOGRAPHS
TRADITIONAL HOME
Best of Showhouse
ROSEMARY BEACH
RICHARD SEXTON

Arts of Ancient Viet Nam

MARRAKESH BY DESIGN
BAZAAR
SO CHIC
STYLE AND SUBSTANCE
Cartier
Spanish Style
The Garden Book
New Seaside Interiors
Paris Interiors
Remodelista
WINDOWS

can ...
WAG-A-LOT

WAG-A-LOT
VISIT WAGALOT.COM
penn
penn
penn
penn

CUENTOS Y CANCIONES DEL ABC
IGGY PECK, ARCHITECT

Giant Book of ANIMAL Facts
HOW TO TEACH YOUR BABY TO SWIM
Alexander Tsiaras from Conception to Birth
THE COMPLETE ADVENTURES OF PETER RABBIT
DAN SAVAGE THE KID
Rookie Dad Susan Fox
La función
SNOWMAN IN AFRICA
MARVEL THE X-MEN MARVEL ENCYCLOPEDIA
ULTIMATE PETER SANDERSON
MYTHOLOGY
SESAME STREET: A CELEBRATION 40 YEARS OF LIFE ON THE STREET
CHARLIE THE RANCH DOG
HOW MANY?
We're Going on a Bear Hunt
600 Black Spots
EVERYONE SAYS I LOVE YOU
This is Hong Kong
香港
The 12 Days of Christmas
GALLOP
ALL THE WAY TO LHASA
FREIGHT TRAIN
SUPER HEROES
TIME FOR BED
OPPOSITES
THE SNOWY DAY
Treasure Hunt
Big Book of Big Trains
Counting Colors
Eating the Alphabet
Hello, Van Gogh!
Hello, Picasso!
Cheerios
KNUFFLE BUNNY

ULTIMATE TROPICAL

WOOD

STEVENSON AND GUY
Vietnamese Ceramics: A Separate Tradition
Art Media Resources
ULTIMATE TROPICAL
R
OBRA INCOMPLETA > VIK MUNIZ < INCOMPLETE WORKS
OBRA INCOMPLETA > VIK MUNIZ < INCOMPLETE WORKS

The Leftovers Tom Perrotta

CHAPTER FIVE:
MODERN MANHATTAN

My mother bravely fought cancer for many years. Around the fifth year of her initial battle the doctors gave us devastating news—while it was believed that surgery and treatment had removed all of the cancer in her body, the originating site had been overlooked and now the cancer was back. By the time the doctors made this discovery it had grown and spread radically. Her last years were very difficult, with multiple rounds of painful chemotherapy and radiation treatments. At some point, she started to fade—when people are that sick and approaching death the person you know sometimes disappears. But I had glimpses of her; she had been a fighter her entire life and we could all tell that she was doing her best to stay with us as long as she could. Sometimes she would rally and the mom I knew would be back if only for a few minutes. Many have experienced this with their loved ones who are in the process of transitioning.

My mother was my best friend. I often took the night shifts in her last months, because someone needed to be awake at all times in case she needed something. She did not want to move to Atlanta and preferred to stay in her own home, in McLean, Virginia. One night, as I was sitting on her bed, she all of sudden opened her eyes and was incredibly present and lucid in a way that she had not been for many days. She looked at me and said, "I want you to know that I love you very much. And I need you to promise me two things. First, you need to promise me that you will have children. Also, you have to promise you will buy a place in New York City." Although we had often discussed the importance of family and she unquestionably knew that I deeply wanted to be a family man, I was a bit taken aback by her request that I purchase property in Manhattan. I had every intention of having a family. But a place in New York City?

My mother always felt that if you were going to be a creative person, especially one in my business, you had to have a presence in Manhattan. She was very savvy and astute. I was not based there, and she was always a little concerned about what I was missing out on by not being in New York more often. Not long after that I had gone to CNN's New York studios, located at Columbus Circle, for a guest appearance. The view from the guest waiting room is breathtaking—all of Columbus Circle as well as Central Park. It's a very unique and beautiful view. I had never been as impressed by a view in Manhattan, so that became my benchmark for a New York apartment. That's what led me to my tiny apartment with an amazing view of Columbus Circle and the park. It took me a while to fulfill that promise to my mom, but I eventually did. I traded space for view and location. Just the advice she would have given me.

I think of her every time we walk into the apartment. She was so right about New York. I have fallen in love with the city, and it doesn't matter that the apartment is small. I had dreams that my Manhattan place would be in a grand pre-war building with high ceilings and intricate moldings. I ended up in a non-descript late 1980's building—but with an unparalleled view. The message here is to understand what's important to you. For me it was that amazing view and a great location. Two things that my mom said you could never change about a home. Don't get stuck on one idea because it might keep you from considering another, better option. Keep your mind open and possibilities will follow.

PAUL STRAND
APERTURE
VISIONS OF PARADISE
CHINA

Andrew Carrington Shelton
INGRES
THE COLLIER CAMPBELL ARCHIVE
ILEX

SCXU 670656 0
BER 2200
SCXU 282104 1
BM 2200
eat.shop nyc
eat.shop chicago
THE SMALL HOUSE BOOK
JEFF KOONS

INBU 2232365
USA 2210
TMRU 2106735

THE HISTORY
OF SURFING
MATT WARSHAW

CHAPTER SIX:
SEA ESCAPE

I discovered Rosemary Beach when I was an intern at my first job out of graduate school. Like most architecture and design students in the country, I had studied its predecessor, Seaside, a master planned community on the Gulf Coast of Florida and perhaps the most important example of an urban planning movement known as New Urbanism. The idea behind Seaside started in 1946, when the grandfather of visionary architect Robert S. Davis bought 80 acres of land along the coast of Northwest Florida. In 1979, Davis inherited the land and began its transformation into a beachside town sympathetic to the architectural vernacular of traditional wood-framed homes of the small town south, with the guidance of town planners and architectural partners Andres Duany and Elizabeth Plater-Zyberk, otherwise known as DPZ.

America was gripped in suburban development at the time, and New Urbanism was an attempt to pull people out of their cars and onto their front porches and sidewalks to engage with their neighbors. The town plan and architectural code was specifically designed to promote face-to-face interaction, creating a sense of community and connectedness that had all but disappeared in suburban America.

Like most young architects and designers at the time, my co-workers and I were obsessed with studying Seaside up close. Despite our meager salaries, we'd often spend our vacations there, renting homes in the community with far fewer beds than could reasonably accommodate our group. On one of those trips, we heard that DPZ was planning a second New Urbanist community that was just breaking ground, called Rosemary Beach. On our way out of town we stopped by the site, which was still mostly land except for a single trailer housing the sales office. The woman in the office was wonderfully gracious in giving us a walking tour of the proposed town, particularly since she knew we were fresh-out-of-school interns and couldn't afford to buy anything at Rosemary Beach.

I kept that dream alive, however. Some of us hatched a ridiculous plan to buy the cheapest lot, dividing the cost ten ways. Even then it would have been out of our financial reach. But I never forgot Rosemary Beach and I was determined to someday have a place there to call my own. For over a decade I actually bought things for this nonexistent beach house—including a dining table, a bed, lighting fixtures, even chargers for dinner plates. I didn't even have chargers for my Atlanta dining room.

After Craig and I got together, we looked at every house in Rosemary Beach that came on the market, dreaming of someday spending school breaks with our kids in this idyllic beach town. After years of looking at countless homes, one of the few unbuilt lots remaining came to our attention. It was a 30-second walk to the beach and an equally close walk to Main Street—accompanied by the possibility of tremendous gulf views!

Moments after discovering this perfect lot, we also discovered that it was under contract with another party. Like the Atlanta house, we were saddened to have lost the perfect situation. And just like the Atlanta house, it miraculously came back on the market. It took me less than a minute to draw the concept of our home on a paper napkin. I knew what it was supposed to look like; I could feel it. As I write this, I am looking out at the Gulf of Mexico from the house that started on a paper napkin. This house is a testament to not giving up on your dreams. It sounds corny, but it is true. That's what I want for you and why I wrote this book—so you can make your home into a place you dream about.

H

WORLD ATLAS AND ENCYCLOPEDIA
Planet Earth AN ILLUSTRATED HISTORY

WEST WATER ST.
TOWN LN.

PART THREE:

APPENDIX

AT-A-GLANCE
CHEAT SHEETS

These reminders bring together the critical measurements for every major space in your house, along with a quick list of questions to bring with you when purchasing wood and upholstered furniture. I hope you find these references handy!

GENERAL FURNITURE ARRANGEMENT DIMENSIONS

- **18″:** Distance between coffee table and sofa
- **12″:** Distance between lounge chair and dedicated ottoman
- **24″:** Distance between centerline of dining chairs
- **24″:** Minimum passage distance between furniture pieces
- **36″:** Ideal passage distance between furniture pieces and through a room
- **12″** to **18″:** Distance between rug edge and closest wall, fireplace hearth, or bump out
- **2″:** Minimum planning distance between furniture pieces or between furniture and wall
- **42″** to **120″:** Minimum to maximum comfortable distance between seating in a conversation group
- **26″** to **84″:** Distance between primary seating and 1080/p televisions 17″ to 54″ diagonal

GENERAL HANGING DIMENSIONS

- **0″:** Curtain hanging height distance to the ceiling (Curtains should be hung as close to the ceiling as possible.)
- **16″** to **18″:** Wall-hung kitchen cabinet height measured from the top of the base cabinet countertop to the lowest point of the wall cabinet.
- **26″:** Toilet paper holder height from finished floor
- **36″** to **48″:** Towel bar height from finished floor
- **75″** to **76″:** Standard shower curtain rod hanging height from finished floor to the rod center (A shower curtain should hang at least 3 to 4 inches above the floor, or 2 inches below the step of a walk-in shower.)
- **48″** to **60″:** Television hanging height from finished floor to the screen center when not above a fireplace mantel.
- **60″:** General picture and mirror hanging height from finished floor to center when not above a fireplace or headboard. When hanging a group of pictures in gallery style, hang the grouping 60″ from finished floor to the center of the group.
- **66″:** Pendant or chandelier height hanging over a table, from finished floor to the lowest point of fixture
- **76″:** Minimum light fixture or ceiling fan height to walk under, from finished floor to the lowest point of fixture for ceilings 114″ inches or lower.
- **84″:** Minimum light fixture or ceiling fan height to walk under, from finished floor to the lowest point of fixture for ceilings 114″ inches or higher.

DINING AREA DIMENSIONS

Table Length or Diameter for Comfortable Seating

Shape	**36″**	**48″**	**54″**	**60″**	**72″**	**84″**	**96″**	**108″**	**120″**
Rectangular	1 to 2	4	n/a*	4 to 6	6 to 8	6 to 8	8 to 10	10	10 to 12
Round or Square	4 to 6	4	6	6 to 8	8 to 10	10 to 12	n/a*	n/a*	n/a*
Oval**	n/a*	n/a*	n/a*	6	6 to 8	8	n/a*	n/a*	n/a*

* Not applicable, as these are non-standard measurements for these shapes of tables.
**Assuming standard depth is 36″ to 42″

Clearance and Distance in Inches to Ensure Maximum Comfort at Table

- **7″:** Between the chair arm and apron of the table
- **12″:** Minimum place setting space in front of each diner at a rectangular table
- **15″:** Maximum centerpiece height to allow diners at the table to see each other
- **26″:** Minimum place setting space in front of each diner at a round table
- **29** to **31″:** Standard height for a dining room table
- **36″:** Minimum distance from the outer edge of a dining table to the edge of the rug underneath
- **48″:** Minimum distance between dining table and an exit
- **54″:** Minimum distance from the table's edge to the nearest wall or piece of furniture, when a chair sits in between; otherwise maintain a minimum distance of 24 to 36 inches
- **66″:** Height of the ceiling light fixture's underside to the finished floor

BEDROOM AREA DIMENSIONS

- **24″:** Minimum passage space around the sides and foot of your bed frame
- **24″** to **25″:** Average bed frame and mattress height
- **17″** to **18″:** Average platform bed and mattress height
- **48″:** Average height of a standard headboard from the floor to the top edge of headboard
- **2″:** Space between your nightstand and your bed
- **25″ or less:** Ideal nightstand depth
- **2″:** The distance higher or lower of your nightstand in relation to the top of your mattress

KITCHEN AREA DIMENSIONS

- **36″:** The most comfortable kitchen counter height for most people to stand and work
- **16″** to **18″:** The ideal clearance distance between the countertop and the lowest point of the wall cabinets
- **16″** to **18″:** The ideal height of a kitchen backsplash area between the countertop and the lowest point of the wall cabinets
- **42″:** Minimum kitchen clearance distance between range and opposite base cabinets
- **36″:** Minimum kitchen clearance distance between dishwasher and opposite base cabinets
- **42″:** Minimum kitchen clearance distance between dishwasher and range on opposing side
- **0″:** Ideal distance between top of wall cabinets and the ceiling if you have ceilings 12 feet or lower

BATHROOM AREA DIMENSIONS

- **29″** and **30″:** Standard height for conventional bathroom countertops
- **33″** to **35″:** Standard height for "back saver" bathroom counters, plus an inch for the countertop
- **75″** to **80″:** Standard height of sconces above bathroom mirrors, measured above the finished floor to the center of the fixture
- **60″** to **65″:** Standard height of sconces on either side of a bathroom mirror measured from finished floor to center of fixture
- **26″** to **28″:** Standard height of a toilet paper holder, to prevent awkward stretching and reaching
- **48″:** Standard height of towel bars
- **29″** to **30″:** Standard height of a bathroom counter when paired with a vessel sink
- **75″** to **76″:** Typical rod hanging height for a standard shower curtain from finished floor to the center of the rod

WOOD FURNITURE: QUESTIONS

- **What is this piece made of?** Is it:
  - Solid wood throughout. If so, is it:
    - Hardwood (preferred) like oak or maple
    - Softwood like pine
  - Real wood veneer. If so, what is the substrate?
    - Wood: Preferred
    - 9-layer or higher plywood
    - Less than 9-layer plywood
    - MDF (medium density fiberboard)
    - OSB (oriented strand board): Avoid
    - Particleboard: Avoid
  - Imitation wood or imitation wood veneer such as a plastic laminate
- **Will this piece be able to be re-sanded and re-finished at some point if I need to?**
- **How is this piece put together? In other words, what are the joints like?**
  - Dovetail
  - Mortise and tenon
  - Dowels
  - Biscuit
  - Butt
- **If the piece has drawers, how are they constructed?** Do they have:
  - Glides
  - Glides and stops
  - Wooden rails
  - Floating bottoms
- **For drawers, what are the bottoms made of?**
  - Solid wood: Preferred
  - Plywood
  - MDF (medium-density fiberboard)
  - OSB (oriented strand board)
  - Particleboard: Avoid
- **How do I maintain the finish on this piece?**

UPHOLSTERED FURNITURE: QUESTIONS

For upholstered furniture such as sofas, loveseats, sectionals, and lounge chairs:

- **What is the frame made of?** Is it:
  - » Kiln-dried hardwood: Preferred
  - » Hardwood plywood
  - » Marine plywood
  - » Softwood: Avoid
- **Is there a spring bed?** Avoid lounge furniture without springs. If there are springs, are they:
  - » Eight-way hand-tied: Preferred
  - » Sinuous S-shaped or sinuous serpentine
  - » Drop-in coil springs
- **What is the board thickness underneath?** Is it:
  - » 1¼" or more: Preferred
  - » 1¼"or less
- **How are the joints and frame assembled?**
  - » Double doweled: Preferred
  - » Single doweled
  - » Tongue and groove
  - » Screwed
  - » Nailed
  - » Stapled: Avoid
- Are there corner blocks? If so, are they:
  - » Glued and screwed: Preferred
  - » Nailed in
  - » Stapled or just glued: Avoid
- How are the legs attached?
  - » Built into the frame: Sturdier
  - » Screwed into the frame: Less sturdy but perhaps more convenient for moving
  - » Glued
- What is the pillow composition? Determine your comfort level, then look for quality. Is it:
  - » High-density foam wrapped with down & feathers: High quality, comfortable for most
  - » High-density foam wrapped with poly-down: Nice quality, comfortable for most
  - » High-density foam wrapped with polyester batting: Nice quality, comfortable for most
  - » Spring down, which is a spring bed wrapped with down: Nice quality, comfortable for most
  - » Down or down & feathers: High quality, soft seat, lumpy appearance
  - » High-density foam: High quality, hard for most
  - » Standard-density foam: Moderate quality, hard for most
  - » Low-density foam: Avoid
  - » Polyester fiber or polyester fill: Avoid

- Are the cushions reversible? This will extend the life of your sofa.
- What is the upholstery fabric made of?
- If you are looking at leather, is it:
  - Genuine leather: Preferred
  - Bonded leather: Generally avoid
- How do I maintain it? Is the fabric treated? If not, is it treatable?
- If there is a slipcover involved, can it be laundered at home? Or does it need to be dry-cleaned?
- Will it be able to make it into the space where I want to put it? Consider:
  - The hard dimensions, excluding removable elements like pillows
  - The dimensions of the intended pathway from A to B in your home, including elevators, stairways, door openings, and hallways
  - If the legs are easily removable
- Is there a warranty? If so, what are the terms?

RESOURCES

APPLIANCES

Dacor
800-793-0093
www.dacor.com

CABINETRY

Omega Cabinetry
612-375-8500
www.omegacabinetry.com

CARPETS & RUGS

Milliken Carpets
Carpets and Rugs
800-241-4826
www.milikenfloors.com

Myers Carpet and Flooring Center
Rugs, Carpeting, Wood
866-450-5551
www.myerscarpet.com

DOOR AND CABINET HARDWARE

Emtek Assa Abloy
800-356-2741
www.emtek.com

FABRIC & TRIM

Calico
800-213-6366
www.calicocorners.com

Trend Fabrics
800-945-3838
www.trend-fabrics.com

FINE ART GALLERIES

Jackson Fine Art
404-233-3739
www.jacksonfineart.com

Sikkema Jenkins & Co.
212-929-2262
www.sikkemajenkinsco.com

FURNITURE & HOME DÉCOR

Anthropologie
800-309-2500
www.anthropologie.com

Boulevard, A Langley Empire Co.
Home Fragrance, Candles, and Décor
888-591-1815
www.langleyempirecandle.com
www.blvddecor.com

The Container Store
Organization & Storage
888-266-8246
www.containerstore.com

Crate & Barrel
800 967 6696
www.crateandbarrel.com

Design Within Reach
800-944-2233
www.dwr.com

The Designer's Workroom
404-355-5080
www.thedesignersworkroomatlanta.com

Frontgate
888-263-9850
www.frontgate.com

Mitchell Gold + Bob Williams
800-489-4195
www.mgbwhome.com

Natuzzi
www.natuzzi.com

RH, Restoration Hardware
800-762-1005
www.rh.com

Room & Board
800-301-9720
www.roomandboard.com

West Elm
888-922-4119
www.westelm.com

William Sonoma Home
877-812-6235
www.wshome.com

LIGHTING

Flambeaux Gas Lanterns
Gas Lanterns
504-881-3054
www.flambeauxlighting.com

Stonegate Designs
Lamps & Lighting Fixtures
269-429-8323
www.stonegatedesigns.com

USA Light and Electric
Recessed Fixtures & Bulbs
877-235-0020
www.usalight.com

PAINT & WALL DÉCOR

Artisan Rooms
Custom Murals & Painting
614-940-4176
www.artisanrooms.com

Benjamin Moore Paint
855-724-6802
www.benjaminmoore.com

Maya Romanoff Corporation
Wall covering
773-465-6909
www.mayaromanoff.com

Sherwin-Williams Paint
800-474-3794
www.sherwin-williams.com

SOLID SURFACES & TILE

Cambria
Natural Quartz Surfaces
866-226-2742
www.cambriausa.com

Ceramic Technics
Ceramic & Natural Stone Tile
770-740-0050
www.ceramictechnics.com

ACKNOWLEDGMENTS

I am a book lover. And anyone who knows me knows that I am a magnet for them. Surrounding myself with books in every room of every house is one of those habits that brings me great comfort but that I'm also conscious of controlling, like eating too much pie, procuring too many objects from world travels, or adopting too many dogs. So finally having my first book published is a meaningful personal milestone. And it wouldn't have happened without the guidance, help, and inspiration from plenty of people who deserve to be acknowledged.

Thanks to my family. You don't get to choose your family in life so I'm especially grateful to have an exceptionally loving one. Mom, Katherine, Rachel, George, Carl, Linda, Bob, Uncle Joe, Aunt Annie, Carmen, Carson, Brooke, Grayson, Dave, Bonnie, Lucy, and Sally: I'm so grateful that you are my tribe.

Thanks to my friends. You do get to choose your friends in life and I've chosen exceptionally well. Mitch, Mia, Lauren D., Bob, Sara, James, Stacie, Paul, Holley, Alyssa, Dan, Rob, Deb, Thomas, Patrick, Matt, Gina, Barry, Jenya, David L., Rumaan, Anne Marie, Brant, Brian J., Ashley, Bill, Ryan, Ross, Mila, Tyler, Nassrin, Kevin, Brock, Brent, Anissa, Holly, Arash, Rebecca, Derk, Darren, Lauren H., Leigh, John, Britton, Olivia, Keith, Whitney, Loren, David S., Margery, Steve, Tanta, Lori, Scott, Kirk, Todd, Caryl, Barron, Charles, Tyler A., Tamar, Leslie, Galen, Greg, Rick, Beth, Haven, Angeli, Ajay, Amita, Tim, Jess, Jen, Michael B., Chris, Heather, Tyler M., SallyAnn, Martha, Cynthia, Sabrina, Steve, Letsa, Jason V., Millie, Sharon, Nina, Jennifer, Rebecca, Emily, David K., and David F.: I'm so grateful to have you in my corner.

Thanks to the exceptional and talented group who helped make this book possible. Jeff Bernstein, Laura Nolan, David A. Land, Karen Kelly, Jennifer Kasius, Josh McDonnell, Kristin Kiser, Kathleen Schmidt, the team at Running Press, David Finer, Bill Carle, David Bowman, Rick Langley, Mercie Ritter, Gail Jameson, Kyle O'Brien, Karla Guatemala, and Matt Gustin: I'm grateful for your hard work and invaluable contributions.

Thanks to those who were willing to lend a hand to a first time author learning the ropes. Michael Clinton, Ellen Levine, Sara Peterson, Rumaan Alam, Christiane Lemieux, and Brant Janeway: I'm grateful for your invaluable advice, insight, and assistance.

And thanks to our four-legged kids. Schmoo, Bob, Hank, Scooter, Lars, and Juno: I'm grateful for all the stress relief.

Most of all, thanks to Craig, Gavin, and Vera. Nothing is worth it without you. Your love reminds me every day what this life is really all about. I'm beyond grateful that we are a family.

For helping to make it possible for me to practice interior design for nearly 25 years, work in television for over 15 years, design hundreds of home products, and create this book, I also want to express my thanks to the fans who've helped open all of these wonderful doors and more. I'm so grateful for your support.

INDEX